THE RECORDED SAYINGS
OF
MA-TSU

THE RECORDED SAYINGS
OF
MA-TSU

Translated from the Dutch
by
Julian F. Pas

Introduced, translated into Dutch and annotated
by Dr. Bavo Lievens

With a preface and commentaries
by Master Nan Huai-chin

The original Dutch edition *Ma-tsu, De Gesprekken*
was published by Het Wereldvenster, Bussum, 1981

Studies in Asian Thought and Religion
Volume 6

The Edwin Mellen Press
Lewiston/Queenston

Library of Congress Cataloging-in-Publication Data

Ma-Tsu, 709-788.
  The recorded sayings of Ma-tsu.

  (Studies in Asian thought and religion ; v. 6)
  Translation of: Ma-tsu, de gesprekken.
  Includes index.
    Zen Buddhism--Early works to 1800. I. Lievens,
Bavo. II. Nan, Huai-chin. III. Title. IV. Series.
BQ9265.M313 1987   294.3'927   87-18536
ISBN 0-88946-058-2

This is volume 6 in the continuing series
Studies in Asian Thought and Religion
Volume 6 ISBN 0-88946-058-2
SATR Series ISBN 0-88946-050-7

All rights reserved. For information contact:

The Edwin Mellen Press   The Edwin Mellen Press
Box 450   Box 67
Lewiston, New York   Queenston, Ontario
USA 14092   L0S 1L0 CANADA

Printed in the United States of America

CONTENTS

ABBREVIATIONS

CTL	Ch'üan-teng lu
DCBT	Dictionary of Chinese Buddhist Terms
HTC	Hsü Tsang Ching
IBK	Indogaku Bukkyogakku kenkyu
LAVS	Lankāvatāra sūtra
MPPS	Mahāprajñāparamitāśāstra
SKSC	Sung kao-seng chuan
T	Taishō Tripitaka
VKN	Vimalakīrtinirdeśa
ZZ	(Dai-Nihon) Zoku-Zokyo (=Jap. for HTC)

THE RECORDED SAYINGS
OF
MA-TSU

FROM THE TRANSLATOR

I am grateful to the University of Saskatchewan's President's Publication Fund for supporting this translation project.

Warm thanks are due to Richard Harris for polishing the English and to Brenda Wotherspoon for her competent word-processing and for preparing the camera-ready copy.

J. F. Pas
Saskatoon, August 1986

FOREWORD

This book is dedicated to Master Nan Huai-chin. His preface was originally in the form of a series of answers to our questions regarding the interpretation of Ch'an Buddhism in the West. Better known as 'Zen', this term covers indeed a variety of ideas which often give rise to divergent misconceptions.

Although quite a number of works have been written about this subject, still too few original texts have been translated and situated in their original context, to enable us to reach a clear understanding of what this Chinese type of Buddhism truly means in itself and could mean in our cultural setting. With the Recorded Sayings of Ma-tsu we hope somehow to fill this gap. For Master Ma-tsu occupies a central position in the transition from the Indian Buddhist meditation tradition to its distinctly Chinese expression, which via Japan has been introduced to the West. From his Sayings and their background may appear to what degree Ch'an Buddhism is linked with the overall Buddhist tradition.

The history of Ch'an Buddhism first of all demonstrates that spiritual awareness is fully dependent on the correct approach, in this case on the authentic Buddhist doctrine and practice, based on the Buddha's own words. Whenever these were not kept in the very centre, each method of Ch'an or Zen as a way to enlightenment has ended in failure. The "golden age of Ch'an" in China was the result of orthodox practice, which with scientific certitude leads up to what no science can suspect.

Ma-tsu's teaching inaugurated for Buddhism a flourishing period which later was never equaled, not

even in Japan. We should not lose sight of the fact
that this type of literature derives from a period and
from communities where insight and effort were more
intense than what we in our time consider as appropriate or even attainable. The next step should therefore
be the practice of this original Ch'an discipline,
which is characterized by a spirit of pragmatic real-
ism.

Without practical approach, each theoretical
acquaintance with an all-embracing and spiritual (i.e.
transcending the duality of our thought-processes)
discipline such as Buddhism, has to remain fruitless.
For its philosophy points toward what is verified
through meditation. Its meditation means openness
toward reality such as it reveals itself. If one takes
ideas for reality, then one mistakes "the pointing
finger for the moon". It is, in other words, the way
of meditation that leads from the finger to the moon.

I acknowledge my gratefulness to Master Nan Huai-
chin, who has answered my questions with infinite
patience and clear simplicity, and to my learned friend
Julian Pas, who spared no effort to make this translation available.

B. Lievens
Taipei, August 1978
Hong Kong, October 1985

PREFACE BY MASTER NAN HUAI-CHIN

Chinese Ch'an Buddhism has sometimes by contemporary authors been represented as "a revolt against Buddhism". As a result the misconception arose that Ch'an Buddhism was a reaction against the original Buddhist doctrine and a rejection of the traditional method of Buddhist practice. Whether we have to do with revolt or innovation, these and similar expressions imply in the ordinary ways of thinking a reactionary character. Hence the misinterpretation of Ch'an Buddhism, because "what one has wrongly passed along, is being accepted by a hundred others"[1]. After the original Buddhist teaching, including all doctrines and practices of both Hīnayāna and Mahāyāna, had been transmitted to China, the Ch'an school developed itself during the Sui-T'ang period (6th to 9th century); it fully accepted all Buddhist tenets and methods of practice. It was purely due to its adaptation to Chinese culture: ideas, customs and character, that also the essence of Confucianism and Taoism was incorporated, with the result that a distinctly Chinese style of teaching was adopted merely as a didactic device. This, however, did not only apply to the Ch'an school; all ten contemporary schools of Buddhism[2], as well as the method of Buddhist research following the 'systematization and sub-division of the doctrine'[3], did not in general, and only with minor variations, abandon the integral acceptance of the Buddha's teaching and practice. This can be illustrated through countless examples: for instance with reference to the Recorded Sayings of Ma-tsu, one could easily point out by means of Buddhist exegesis, that no statement is not in accordance with a doctrinal reference in the

Buddhist Scriptures. This, however, would necessitate a separate study.

To say it in simple and clear terms, the masters of the Ch'an school always honoured the famous saying: "if one commands the school but not the teaching, one talks nonsense as soon as one opens the mouth; if one commands the teaching but not the school, one resembles a one-eyed dragon".[4] Or, as Ch'an master Yung-chia says in his Hymn on Realization: "if one commands the school as well as the teaching, concentration and wisdom are perfect and clear and one does not get stuck in emptiness".[5] This is certainly the best clarification, although certain contemporary academics hold that Yung-chia's hymn, on the basis of critical source examination, is subject to doubt; thus one gets more and more entangled. Here a statement of the Ch'an masters is most appropriate: "all things are originally at ease, it is only man who looks for trouble"!

At the root of Western misconceptions about Ch'an Buddhism there obviously still is a more remote cause, the study of Buddhism in Europe after the 17th century. The original source materials concerning early Buddhism were not any longer available, and one was principally thrown on the Southern Hīnayāna Buddhism and the Buddhist Pali literature. Add to this that during the 18th and 19th centuries, in part consciously, in part unconsciously, Chinese culture was explicitly rejected and disparaged with the result that the major part of authentic data concerning Chinese Buddhism was ignored. Moreover, after World War II the study of Zen was introduced to Europe and America from Japan. One is, however, well aware that Japanese scientific research in the area of the so-called Oriental culture, including Chinese culture, since the Meiji restoration

(1868-1912) consciously or unconsciously continued the Western approach. As well as in the West, this research was handicapped due to nationalistic and political factors.

Under such circumstances the true spirit of Ch'an Buddhism totally degenerated. One may also consider this as an expression of the general tendency in human history which leads toward decline of culture; and this can in no way be remedied.

The interpretation of Ch'an Buddhism, as if the various religious schools would deny and oppose each other, is a serious problem for the comparative philosophical study of Buddhism. It can be generally stated that different people may reach totally disparate conclusions because their initial standpoint is different. It is, however, my opinion, and this does not only affect the Buddhist systems, that if one leaves aside all institutional frameworks and particular methods of instruction, all religions in their transcendental spirit are mutually in harmony, and can even complement and clarify each other. There is, indeed, only one truth, as the Buddha signified with his 'non-duality' (no-second teaching), followed up by the Ch'an masters with their statement, "outside this one reality, each second one is not true".

Buddhism in China, as far as it was seriously adhered to, and no matter whether one practiced Hīnayāna or Mahāyāna, has always explicitly and exclusively pursued the goal of realization. The methods of realization, based on the study of the doctrine, are from beginning to end in principle never to be separated from the **sūtras**, the **vinaya** and the commentaries.[6] The method of practice, whether in Hīnayāna or Mahāyāna, have always the four **dhyānas** and the eight **samādhis** as

their basis.[7]   Before the Sui-T'ang period (589-907)
the Mahāyāna scriptures had not yet reached universal
circulation, and as a result the Hīnayāna method of
meditation practice enjoyed greater popularity. In the
middle of the T'ang dynasty, not only the Ch'an school
came to its full development, but it was also due to
the simultaneous rise of the other schools, that the
Mahāyāna method of meditation gained general acceptance. From a doctrinal viewpoint one may classify
within the Mahāyāna tradition of meditation two types
of later Ch'an developments, called **'dhyāna** of the
Tathāgata' and **'dhyāna** of the masters-patriarchs'.[8]

The meditation practice of the Small Vehicle is
based on the Hīnayāna doctrine: through the exclusion
of the sensuous world within and without mind and body,
and through the undivided attentive guarding of one's
concentration in heart and mind, one realizes liberation from attachment to the material world in an autonomous sublimation. Numerous have been the expressions
of forceful energy with such results as the attainment
of super-sensuous faculties, or 'liberation while
sitting and death while standing' and similar conditioned achievements on the boundaries of life and
death. To use a more concrete comparison, the Hīnayāna
method of meditation practice is directed toward the
gradual converging of the confused and disconnected
into one point of concentration, after which it is
again discarded to remain forever in a state of quiet
emptiness and purity.[9] The Mahāyāna method is equally
based on the teachings of the Hīnayāna as of the
Mahāyāna; each point or aspect of consciousness is
immediately from within its centre as through an explo-
sion destroyed so that its ultimate emptiness becomes
clearly and independently present.

In the Ch'an school of Ma-tsu's time (709-789) the observation of rules and regulations was rather strict. During the flourishing period of Buddhism in the T'ang dynasty, three degrees were distinguished: the Hīnayāna regulations applicable to novices, those applicable to monks, and the bodhisattva rules of Mahāyāna. The monks of the Ch'an school, however, mostly followed the **Fourfold Vinaya**.[10] With regard to the Mahāyāna bodhisattva discipline, in China one most often followed the Brahmajālasūtra,[11] whereas in Tibet the Vinaya text contained in bodhisattva Maitreya's Yogācārabhūmiśāstra was generally adhered to.[12] Among the sutras popular in the school of that period, the Diamond sūtra, a prajñāpāramitā text[13], mostly served as a basis for beginners. For that reason, the Ch'an school has later also been called the 'Prajñā School', as well as 'Bodhidharma-' and 'Lanka School'. The great Ch'an masters, however, continued to emphasize the Lankāvatārasūtra,[14] the Vimalakīrtinirdeśa,[15] the Nirvānasūtra,[16] the Lotus-sūtra[17] and other texts. Quite a number of masters from the five post-Matsu Ch'an schools, such as the Lin-chi School and the Fa-yen School, were moreover also great teachers in the Yogācāra School[18] or the 'Consciousness-only' School.

What then were the characteristics of the Ch'an school? To explain it in a simple way: the highest Buddhist teaching of the mind, the complicated and detailed analytical method to realize the transcendent Path (**Tao**), was being reduced to the simplicity of every day living, and could be realized in the middle of ordinary things. In this way the Ch'an school has contributed to the spread of Buddhism all over China, to its penetration into all levels of the population; it made Buddhism occupy a central position in Chinese

culture, and caused its deep roots and sturdy branches
to be transmitted from generation to generation. This
metamorphosis, however, of the highest and transcendent
Path, which was seen to manifest itself spontaneously
in ordinary every day life, also gave rise to a later
wave of Ch'an 'maniacs', or the 'prattle-Ch'an' of
beginners, who keep talking of realization without
realizing anything yet, and of enlightenment without
seeing any light!   This became during the Sung period
(960-1279) a stimulus for Neo-Confucianism to react
with strict rationalism against the shortcomings of
such a superficial 'maniacal Ch'an'. From the end of
the Ming period (1368-1644), this kind of reaction
turned into empty fanaticism.   Such excesses are the
unavoidable products of old and new spiritual currents,
in China as well as elsewhere.

The popularization of Ch'an Buddhism is closely
linked with the fact that the great masters around
Ma-tsu's time formulated the Buddhist doctrine in the
most current vernacular and thus unlocked its mysterious technical terminology. In this way originated the
new literary style of **recorded sayings**[19] in Buddhist
literature, extremely realistic in style, and extremely
lively in content. The masters of the Ch'an school
usually gave to the Buddha's proclamation an authentic
and concrete interpretation, based on every day facts
and matters and with our personal experience as a
starting point. These recorded sayings of the Ch'an
masters on the one hand and the learned theoretical
treatises and commentaries on the other hand, have each
their own advantages.

The **kung-an** (in Japanese **koan**)[20] of the Ch'an
school are different from the recorded sayings.   The
latter have a very clear central theme, the Ch'an

masters' words about 'reality'. The **kung-an** on the contrary contain the 'events'[21] and the deeds from the masters' biographies. They narrate for example on what occasion the master started to foster doubts and to search for the ultimate meaning of man and his world. Or they mention under what circumstances or on hearing what words they obtained insight into the highest truth and what crucial awakenings they experienced in the course of their religious training, etc. Although the **kung-an** at first sight are merely narrative testimonies of certain events with content, they still present a dynamic study of the learning processes and experiences of the early masters. They even serve as guidelines and stimulation for later disciplines and offer an effective assistance for verifying one's own insight.

As a result of the popularization and the use of the vernacular in the recorded sayings and the **kung-an**, they made a more profound impression upon the scholars and were more easily accepted. This is one of the reasons why Ch'an Buddhism after Ma-tsu enjoyed such a general propagation.

After a period of silence, Ch'an Buddhism today occupies once more a position of great attention even in Europe and America. The answer to the question in how far Ch'an may be 'good tidings' for Westerners, is optimistic. Ch'an Buddhism is a religious trend which "directly points to man's spirit, in order to see his own nature and to become enlightened". Buddhism with its exalted and profound doctrine of the Transcendent Path, and its concrete methods of practice and realization, had in the course of time developed into a great number of schools and became entangled in many different doctrinal propositions. Under those circumstances Ch'an Buddhism reacted by discarding the limitations of the tradition and letting its genial spirit gush forth with irresistible power. Since its primary and immediate concern was to establish without sidetracks the unique reality of the spirit "which is able to transform matter", it aimed at spiritual realization, which is the emancipation into total independence by reaching the highest wisdom.

The Ch'an method of instruction and disposition make the impression of being non-religious, non-philosophical and non-scientific. But precisely because it guarantees emancipation toward independence and profound wisdom, it is in a position to give integrating answers to religion, philosophy and science. In other words, it is only through a disposition and methods of realization such as Ch'an Buddhism puts forward, that man can really extricate himself from the dead-end of material desires so as to reach a state of authentic spiritualization. In a world in which humanity is submerged in material prosperity and reason is deluded by desire, Ch'an presents an infallible cure as well as a wonderful refreshment.

Taipei,
July, 1978.

PART I - INTRODUCTION

THE SPIRIT OF CH'AN

Ch'an is a Chinese appellation to express the essence of Buddhism. The term, derived from **ch'an-na**, is a transliteration of the Sanskrit **dhyāna**, and is pronounced **zen** in Japanese. It originally points to the Buddhist practice of meditation and more precisely to the four stages of **dhyāna** or absorption. Today the term **ch'an** usually indicates the Chinese direction taken by Buddhism which developed from the Indian **dhyāna** practice.

Like prayer for Christianity, so is meditation the heart of the Buddhist experience. The practice of meditation is, however, not typical of Buddhism, but is rather a universal method found in all great spiritual traditions. In Buddhist meditation the aim is "wisdom" by which it is distinct from other religions; therefore it may also be called "philosophy" ("love of wisdom") in the original sense. Yet, Buddhism is not "thought"; its method leads toward an immediate seeing of absolute truth, which cannot possibly be realized through the medium of thought.

"Wisdom", which in Buddhism is described as "awareness which sees Reality as it is", is born from concentration, in the sense of clear attentiveness. Without concentration there is no "wisdom". Power of concentration is born from a correct way of living. Insight into the mechanics of the human spirit has produced into a set of rules and spiritual exercises, which are an essential factor in the discovery of ultimate truth. Likewise, the purpose of all command-

ments and prohibitions, rules of life and prescriptions
of Buddhism, such as poverty and celibacy, is to elicit, to develop and to protect the power of concentration. They are primary conditions to enable the development of the spirit's sensitivity and sharpness.
Concentration is the instrument through which the
empirical quest for ultimate reality can be performed.
What counts here is the systematic approach of each
scientific discipline. Therefore belief in Buddhism
goes hand in hand with the certainty that each tenet
does indeed correspond with the living reality and that
each method does indeed lead up to its experiential
recognition. (One loves to call Buddhism "the science
of science"). This belief, which does not leave any
doubt or question unsolved or unanswered, is the "moth-
er of wisdom". Ignorance is the root of all human
imperfection. Wisdom leads to perfect liberation. On
this path a man like all of us has preceded us, the
"Buddha" or "Enlightened One". During forty-five years
he proclaimed the "Path" in various ways for various
listeners.

"The proclamation of the Buddha has mind as essence and no-method as method". This is the classic
saying quoted by Ma-tsu to define Ch'an Buddhism.
"Ch'an is the name of mind, mind is the substance of
Ch'an". Ch'an is the final nucleus of the Buddha's
doctrine, and its method is the without-method, i.e.
immediate. The Ch'an school "points directly to the
mind in order to perceive one's original nature and to
become a Buddha".

The "understanding of mind" and the "direct method" of the Ch'an school have, however, also been the
occasion of misunderstandings concerning this "mind"
and the path toward its recognition. For instance,

sudden enlightenment does not at all mean that nothing
is presupposed. Enlightenment is in Ch'an texts often
compared with a flower, and a flower presupposes a stem
and a root. Dhyāna is not only the phonetic (etymolog-
ical) origin but also the root of Ch'an. There is no
sudden enlightenment without gradual cultivation, and
no gradual cultivation without sudden enlightenment.

The Buddhist Path to enlightenment consists of a
trinity: insight, cultivation, action. Insight is to
see the truth (comparable to the discovery of a gold
mine); cultivation is the constant drill in concentration and meditation or the realization of truth (comparable to the exploiting of a gold mine); action is the
behaviour and the carrying out in the world (comparable
to the marketing of the gold). These three sustain and
fertilize each other. There is no wisdom without cultivation and without action. The real cultivation only
starts after gaining insight, when the ego and its ex-
ertions have disappeared. True action follows enlightenment. Without the merits and the virtues of action
(called 'good roots') all knowledge and cultivation
remain fruitless. These are the three pillars on which
rests every authentic spiritual awareness: right insight, right cultivation and right action.

The history of Buddhism shows two major directions: the 'Lower Course' or the 'Small Vehicle'
(Hīnayāna) and the 'Higher Course' or the 'Great Vehicle' (Mahāyāna). In early Buddhism the Small Vehicle
was developed, emphasizing cultivation of self-realization. Later the Great Vehicle manifested itself with
the emphasis on the non-dualistic truth and action-in-
the-world. The practice of dhyāna strictly speaking
belongs to the Lower Course and is the basis of the
Higher Course. The Chinese Ch'an school belongs to

Mahāyāna Buddhism and is the fruit of the Hīnayāna methods of cultivation.

The practice of **dhyāna** starts with preparatory exercises in concentration, for instance with the fixing of one's attention on the in- and out- breathing. The purpose is to widen one's consciousness by concentrating one's attention on one point (just like sunlight does not diminish when concentrated through a magnifying glass into one focal point). In accordance with the talents and situation of each practitioner, there is a variety of methods of concentration, visualization and contemplation, which all aim at the gradual emancipation from 'the world of desire' i.e. the sensuous sphere in which we live.

The fruit of this practice is the entering into a more subtle world, 'the sphere of pure form', which is accompanied by an unmistakable physical and mental transformation: one is in the first stage of meditation or the first **dhyāna**. This and the three subsequent **dhyānas** are reached in a state of perfect concentration and lucidity, in which all sensuous and psychic reactions are dissolved—this is called **samādhi**.

During these four stages of **dhyāna**, one is successively absorbed in the eighteen heavens of the 'world of form'. In the fourth **dhyāna**, during which the Buddha became enlightened, one disposes of supernatural abilities, such as the 'miraculous powers' (power of self-multiplication; power of subtility by which one can penetrate matter as if it were air; power of walking on water, etc.); the 'divine eye' and the 'divine ear'; the knowledge of other beings' consciousness; the remembrance of previous lifetimes, etc. One is then not yet totally independent from the laws and circumstances of the universe (for instance, with the disap-

pearance of the world, the **dhyāna** also disappears).
After the four **dhyānas** of the 'world of form', follow
the four concentrations of the 'world of formlessness'.

This process of meditation practice, mostly called
'the four **dhyānas** and the eight concentrations (or
samādhis)' follows a systematic sequence, which charac-
terizes all real liberation from conditioned existence.
Without this concrete, gradual realization, in which
also the body is 'reborn', no insight is founded and
final. On the other hand, **dhyāna** is a conditioned
practice within the sphere of cause and effect, which,
although indispensable and effective, yet does not
leave the immanence of the three forementioned worlds,
i.e. the total world. Ch'an therefore cannot be reduced to **dhyāna** or to any kind of experience, state or
transformation. All phenomena, which appear in the
mind, are not the mind. "Even if one knows emptiness,
one does not yet know the knower". Final insight is
essentially unconditioned, non-dualistic and immediate.
In practice it may arise from each of the numerous
meditations. It presupposes, however, a preceding
de-conditioning, a power of concentration and wisdom,
which may not just be acquired within this life
time. "Tao follows nature".

The Indian founder of Ch'an Buddhism, the patriarch Bodhidharma, went to China toward the end of the
fifth century. At that time there was within the
intellectual circles of China a genuine interest in
Buddhism, limited as it was to translation issues and
philosophical discussion, and influenced by Taoist
interpretations. Understanding of Mahāyāna doctrine
had found a general acceptance, but was still separated
from realization due to lack of the real process of
practice. Only a small minority devoted itself to the

practice of Hīnayāna methods, and even here the ultimate step from conditioned exercises to the transcendent Tao was missing. Even the great Indian masters
like Kumārajīva, who formerly had interpreted the
highest Mahāyāna doctrine, were themselves practitioners of Hīnayāna methods.

Bodhidharma went to China because he felt that
people there had a talent for the Great Vehicle. Yet
he sat nine years in meditation facing a wall, waiting
for his first disciple. Only after this candidate had
cut off his arm to prove his serious determination, did
Bodhidharma start to teach him 'quietude of mind'.
"When external conditions have ceased and one inwardly
is without desire (attachment), the mind becomes as a
wall, and one can enter the Tao".

Although the original annals are mostly legendary,
still it nowhere appears from them that there is such a
thing as 'sudden awakening' (in Japanese: satori) without a gradual practice; nor is there anything like
enlightenment after which one stops practicing. Moreover, Bodhidharma's Ch'an and that of the patriarchs
after him, was integrally linked with all the aspects
of Buddhist doctrine. The fact that he indicated the
Lankāvatāra sūtra as a guidance toward the realization
of the 'mind-ground', is an unmistakable indication of
the central importance of the practice of meditation in
the original Ch'an school.

The doctrine which Bodhidharma proclaimed was a
summary of the Hīnayāna and Mahāyāna sutras: "There
are many paths to enter the Tao, but they all end up at
two gateways: the gateway of truth and the gateway of
practice". The gateway of truth presupposes the thorough understanding of the doctrine in all its aspects,
the awakening to its spirit, and the deep faith in the

true nature which all beings from themselves originally and perfectly have in common, but which have been obscured through illusions and passions. When opinions and mental constructs have made place for a return to truth and the simplicity of living reality; when one is unshakable and resolutely established in meditation with a spirit as a wall between outer factors and inner tendencies; when one is no longer dependent upon texts and their interpretation, but without sidetracks has been reconciliated with 'the whole truth'; when one acquiesces in the silence of the unconditioned and thus has become one with the inner essence of the teaching, only then can we talk of entering through the gate of truth, according to Bodhidharma.

Original Ch'an Buddhism is thus not at all removed from the scriptural teaching and presents the essence of the Buddha's teaching as only accessible through the traditional practice of **dhyāna**. On the other hand, the practice is only a transition to the absolute truth of the teaching. The **dhyānas** and **samādhis** merely bring about the 'fruits' of the Small Vehicle, and are not the essence of Ch'an.[1] If one appreciates meditation only in view of one's own realization, one may, in the end, be able to reach 'one-sided emptiness' or 'imperfect **nirvāna**'" this, however, is not yet the 'true emptiness' or 'wonderful fullness' of the **Great Nirvāna**.[2] Even if one is established in meditation as a wall, as long as one has not yet entered the essence of the teaching through an awakening, one cannot yet come up to Bodhidharma's first gateway.

The second gateway: the practice of action, not only offers the quintessence of Ch'an Buddhism, but moreover also constitutes the only link which could connect Buddhism with Chinese culture. Here we also find a fundamental similarity with Christianity. This gate summarizes the view of life of both Hīnayāna and Mahāyāna; the basic analytical self-examination not only aims at the purification and perfection of one's own mental and social attitude, but also at the liberation and full realization of all beings. Without the transcendental faculties and abilities, which issue forth from this all-embracing servitude, the maturation towards the 'perfect fruit' of Buddhahood is excluded.

"Whoever on account of an experience or a sudden insight considers his situation of more or less understanding as Ch'an, and as a result carelessly and effortlessly goes his own way and thinks to be self-enlightened, will sooner or later lapse into a state of 'the parrot-prate Ch'an of braggers and free-thinkers'. One chooses the easiest way and has no concern about how to grow in love and service, once one reaches 'the spiritual tranquility by which one would be able to enter the Path'. One loves to read the sayings of the Ch'an masters and thinks that the essence of Ch'an can be found in the **koan** literature.[3] Thereby one looses out of sight the masters' basic words and deeds and their authentic spirit and goes astray on the sidetracks of Ch'an".[4]

This gateway of practice embraces 'the four actions': to pay off all one's debts, to obey one's destiny, to be detached from everything and to act in accordance with the **Dharma**. Whoever applies himself to the Path, must first adopt the correct attitude to life. Life in this world to him means the paying off of all debts. First of all there is one's own debt; there is nothing which he does not owe to others. Nobody owes him anything. Even if he did not do any evil in this life, still he has to bear the consequences of previous life times. There is no coincidence and everything has its cause. Therefore he never worries about what happens to him, since he understands. By leading a life of self-forgetting sacrifice and by returning evil with good, he also releases others from their guilt. Bodhidharma illustrated this through his own life; being poisoned five times and after appointing his successor, he died of it without one word of complaint. In this the true philosopher and the authentic religious person reveals himself. Thus Socrates drank the cup of poison and thus Jesus died on the cross. The attitude of the realized man (arhat) in Hīnayāna Buddhism is: "my life has been completed, holiness has been established; I have fulfilled everything and will not be reborn again". Ch'an master Yung-chia said: "If one understands, all karmic obstacles are seen as originally empty; if one does not understand yet, one has first to pay off one's debts".

Buddhism postulates the emptiness of all things, man and the world. All phenomena are impermanent, they arise and perish through causes and circumstances. Nothing has an autonomous nature. Emptiness is the true reality of all that arises and all that arises has emptiness as its nature. In all this there is no 'I', nor anything that is permanent. Joy and sorrow, prosperity and adversity, honour and shame, grace and disgrace are all the result of previous attitudes and deeds. They appear as in a dream without real significance. When the force of karma is exhausted, the results in which I now rejoice or not, disappear of their own accord. The basic nature does not know any gain or loss, therefore the Ch'an masters urge 'to let go and to obey one's destiny', 'dissolve the old karma and not to create new karma'. This is also the spirit of Lao-tzu, Confucius and the I Ching.

To follow one's destiny is the natural way of Tao, and to act without strife is the 'non-action' of Tao. People of-the-world are always pursuing something and attached to something; because they are attached, they pursue in endless confusion. The sage is not of-the-world because he is not attached to things which arise and again perish. Wherever there is pursuing and attachment, there also is frustration and pain for what is empty, for what is not attained and for what is lost. Truth and joy consist exactly in the ceasing of strife, including self-realization. "Whoever seeks for the **Dharma**, should not seek anything". Whoever wants to understand Ch'an must first of all learn to see how life and body in the world develop according to the law of cause and effect. His only striving is to let the old karma work itself out, therefore he is grateful for everything that happens to him. Here again Lao-tzu's saying "Tao follows its nature" is valid.

'To act in accordance with the **Dharma**' is to act according to the Buddhist principles. Besides obtaining insight into the emptiness of man and world, and liberation through transcendental wisdom, the **arhat** becomes a **bodhisattva** (a being of enlightenment), only motivated by love in order to emancipate all beings in this and other world-systems; this is the bodhisattva vow 'not to enter into ultimate **nirvāna** as long as there is one being not yet emancipated'.

This is the true and correct action of all those who apply themselves to Buddhism. No matter how the Ch'an schools would develop in later times, "anything which does not conform to the 'four actions' of Bodhidharma's original Ch'an, has to be definitely considered as an aberration. There is not the slightest doubt

about this. On the other hand, if spiritual cultivation is truly based on this action, then all rules,
concentration and wisdom are contained in it."[5] Spiritual awareness misses its deepest power when it dis-
cards the wailing and suffering of the world. From
true introspection, the non-being-of-the-world, is born
'extrospection', the being-in-the-world with unlimited
loving compassion. Only within the bodhisattva-per-
spective of the Great Vehicle, is there the prospect of
the 'right, perfect and unsurpassable Enlightenment'.

Bodhidharma made the prophecy that within two
hundred years after his death Ch'an Buddhism would
spread all around. "The number of those who understand
the Path and proclaim the truth will be great, but the
number of those who practice the Path and fathom the
truth minimal". Until the first half of the 8th century his Ch'an school remained limited to a number of
'practitioners of the Path', who in the mountains led
ascetic lives. Thanks to the consistent meditation
practice according to Hīnayāna methods, the number of
'realized ones' was considerable. Thus started an
impressive movement, by which toward the end of the 9th
century Ch'an Buddhism became popular all over China.
In a manner till then unknown but meeting with general
success, the Ch'an masters pointed out the ultimate
significance of Buddhist teaching and cultivation. The
profound and complicated terminology used to approach
the transcendent Path, received an extremely vivid,
direct and simple expression. In ordinary every day
language and in every day life, the essence of the
Buddha's teaching was being presented as a universal
and living reality. In this way the typically Chinese
Ch'an method of teaching originated: on the one hand,
the point of gravity shifted from the scriptural tradi-

tion toward the living audience, while on the other hand there was another shift from doctrinal interpretation toward the vital testimony of those who had realized the teaching. This new method of instruction, in terms of concrete human beings, introduced the vernacular into Buddhism and found its expression in the new literary genre (style) of the Ch'an literature: 'the Recorded Sayings of the Ch'an masters'.

This metamorphosis of the Buddhist proclamation was not only the fruit of a centuries old tradition, but also of new political, social and cultural factors. In the new type of instruction, the whole Buddhist tradition is supposedly known and practiced, and therefore the immediate insight is of central importance, whereas the practice is not often emphasized. Indeed it originated in those circles of monks where all the emphasis was placed on cultivation and realization, and where, according to our standards, a superhuman effort was considered to be a matter of course. It also followed from the practical Chinese way of life, which, having realized the essence of Buddhism, did not consider it indissolubly attached to traditional philosophical and religious formations. In this, however, the Buddhist tradition was being respected by actually denying it in an equally Buddhist fashion. Buddhism implicitly contained in itself the principles of desacralization of its own religion. Sutras and commentaries point out that the 'whole truth' is at stake: the unconditioned, non-dualistic true reality can never be reduced to conditioned, dualistic and tentative forms of religion. These are 'means of salvation' which, although orthodox and effective, yet merely play a preparatory and methodical role. "When the fish has been caught, the net is abandoned", or, in the Buddha's own words: "when one has   reached the opposite   bank, the raft is discarded" (not sooner, however...).

The   ingenious   simplicity   of   the   distinctively Chinese Ch'an Buddhism, which spontaneously followed from the   realization of the highest   truth, was   also responsible for the dangers of its gradual   fossiliza- tion. The original words and deeds of the Ch'an   mas- ters, always gushing forth from a thorough knowledge and practice of the Buddha's teaching, became more and more detached from their original context.   Insight became emphasized at the expense of practice.   The recorded sayings which resulted in the **koan** literature, became nourishment for those who were after insight, without devoting themselves to authentic practice and realization. This should not prevent us, however, from respecting the true spirit of Ch'an Buddhism.

MA-TSU (709-788) AND THE HUNG-CHOU SCHOOL

The formation and spread of the specifically Chinese Ch'an Buddhism in the second half of the 8th century started with Ma-tsu.[6] As a genial educator he contributed to the teaching method, which caused waves of resonance first all over China, later also in Japan and even today in the West. "The name Ch'an or Zen Buddhism receives a clearly definable content only with Ma-tsu, and the transition period between primitive Ch'an Buddhism and the florescence of the proper Ch'an school, coincides with the final years of his life."[7] "All the early Buddhist masters, about whom a typical Ch'an teaching has been transmitted, belong to the Ma-tsu school, and the recording of their sayings started with him. This literature constitutes the major source material for the history of Ch'an Buddhism in that period. It is only starting with Ma-tsu and in relation to his school, that one can talk of a more or less clearly defined history."[8]

Ma-tsu himself has not written anything, and, in contrast to other Ch'an masters of his time, he has not made any effort in the area of evangelism or propaganda. Still he had more than eight hundred known followers and about a thousand unknown disciples. He trained some eighty 'good masters', whose names and first encounters with Ma-tsu have been transmitted in historical sources. These successors spread themselves all over the Chinese territory and did not, like most of their contemporaries, choose as their centres the capital or some famous mountain. "Since these successors in turn founded their own schools, one can say that the great popularity of Ch'an Buddhism is to be directly attributed to Ma-tsu."[9] This wide spread inaugurated the 'golden age of Ch'an and became a culminating point of Chinese culture.

Ma-tsu's teaching presented an inartificial and vital revelation, which cut through the rigidity of a conventional and antiquated religion. Official Buddhism of that time was indeed immobilized in a dead-end, in that the Buddha's teaching had become entangled in scholasticism and in the dogmatic explanations of the scriptures. Even the practice of meditation faced the danger of sinking into technical irrelevancies. Thus we notice that Ma-tsu in his instructions (sections 2-4), time and again points to the true nature of practice and to the ultimate implications of enlightenment. In his dialogues (sections 5-33) we often see appear teachers and preachers who represent the conventional way of instruction. Their impressive scholarship is usually encountered with paradoxical statements or non-logical reactions, which make them suddenly awaken to the true meaning of all exegesis and scholasticism. Thus Ma-tsu developed a direct and powerful teaching method which in numerous original and creative ways revealed the essence of the Buddha's proclamation as a living presence in the context of daily life. In this he also integrated the essence of the Confucian and Taoist traditions, which in his own words and deeds found perfect expression. Let us think for example of Confucius' saying: "the absolute is expressed in the average", of Chuang-tzu's "Tao is in excrement" and of Vimalakīrti's "the lotus flower (symbol of enlightenment) does not prosper on a high plateau, but blossoms in the marshland". Like contemporary poetry which reached a peak in Chinese literature, his teaching radiated with pure simplicity and inner nobility, his dialogues are sparklingly alive and overflow with humor. This indeed introduced 'a new spring and a new sound' into Chinese Buddhist literature.

The renewal movement which issued from Ma-tsu's Ch'an took place in a period of general renewal, characterized by a popularizing tendency, a democratizing of culture and religion. It was moreover enhanced by political factors. The position of the imperial court was in obvious decline, whereas the power of military governors was steadily increasing. Thus Ma-tsu's disciple Lu Ssu-kung[10], an influential political figure, contributed considerably to his master's reputation and to the influence of his movement. Ma-tsu's Ch'an school therefore was no exception to the rule that religion and politics go hand in hand. The centre of Buddhist activity had been replaced toward Kiangsi and Hunan, two remote southern provinces, where the political situation was more stable than in Northern China. This was an important factor in the development of the **dhyāna** practice, which is naturally stimulated in a quieter climate.

Ma-tsu's new teaching method was at first nothing more than spontaneous and situational didactics which strongly appealed to the practical spirit of the Chinese. What was for him only a question of casual and playful circumstance would later turn into the so-called 'secularization' of Ch'an Buddhism. He himself and his successors, however, were authentic masters who did not deviate even one inch from the Buddhist tradition. In the Ch'an school of Ma-tsu's time strong emphasis was placed on the practice of meditation according to the Yoga manuals of the Hīnayāna and on the observance of the rules of religious life according to the Vinaya. The Ch'an masters were furthermore solidly established in the classical systems of Bud-

dhist philosophy. This is quite obvious from the Ch'an
biographies and Ch'an instructions.[11] It is a matter
of course that for instance a box on the ears or the
observation of flying ducks cannot be the cause of enlightenment. Although similar situations can give rise
to a sudden awakening, yet they are nothing more but
the coincidence of circumstances which owe their effec-
tiveness to preceeding discipline. These typical Ch'an
stories are only loose recordings of crucial moments in
the learning process of the elders, and have only value
inasmuch as their context and their referential nature
are recognized.

Ma-tsu's followers considered him to be an orthodox innovator, which resulted into a Ch'an school
called after the region in which he finally established
himself: the Hung-chou School. His successors were
conscious of their own orthodoxy and of the founder's
authority. This appears for instance from <u>The Recorded
Sayings</u> of Lin-chi[12], the most famous among Ma-tsu's
successors, who on the one hand behaves as an unex-
celled iconoclast, and on the other hand appeals to his
successors' authority up to Ma-tsu. Another proof is
the fact that Ma-tsu's immediate successor Pai-chang[13]
composed a detailed 'Rule', which served as a base for
all later communities of Ch'an monks. Ch'an master
Tao-i from Kiangsi was also called 'Ma-tsu', i.e.
'Patriarch Ma' in imitation of the Indian and Chinese
patriarchs since the Buddha himself up to Liu-tsu, the
Sixth Patriarch[14].

The earliest sources about Buddhism in Ma-tsu's
time are the Tun-huang manuscripts. They remain,
however, silent about Ma-tsu and his followers, while
they contain numerous other texts concerning Ch'an
Buddhism in that time period. The reason of it lies in

the fact that the new Ch'an literature: 'the Recorded Sayings of the Ch'an Masters', was at first not taken seriously and was not included in the classical Buddhist literature. Japanese monks who visited China at that time did equally not even mention these texts whereas they did collect other contemporary Ch'an writings.[15] It was only centuries later during the Kamakura period (1135-1333) that the typical Ch'an literature was carried to Japan. The reason was that "the Buddhism of Ma-tsu and his Hung-chou School was too original and too Chinese to be acceptable and digestible for the Japanese."[16]

The first source for Ch'an Buddhism in Ma-tsu's time is the work of Tsung-mi.[17] He was a versatile scholar and a Buddhist monk, who, as the last patriarch of the Huayen School as well as of Shen-hui's Ch'an School (i.e. the Ho-tse School) was highly respected. In his extensive writings, of which a great part has been lost, one finds descriptions of Ch'an Buddhism from Bodhidharma up to his own time. He subdivides the various directions into Seven Houses, Ten Chambers and Five Sects. On the basis of their doctrines, he concludes that there are four schools: The Niu-t'ou School, the Northern School, and the two Southern Schools of Ho-tse and Hung-chou. The Ho-tse School, of which he represented the fifth generation, he considers to be the orthodox successor of Bodhidharma. The intention of his writings is to expose the Hung-chou School as the heterodox one. In that work only Ma-tsu is mentioned, not his successors, whereas the Hung-chou School, under the leadership of Huang-po[18] and Kui-shan[19] had already become the most influential branch of Ch'an Buddhism. In another work he describes the viewpoint of the Hung-chou School as follows: "The

rise of thoughts and the movement of the attention, the
snapping of the fingers or the turning of the eyes,
whatever one does is a function of the Buddha nature,
and that which speaks and acts is nothing but the
Buddha nature." Concerning the Ch'an literature, i.e.
the Recorded Sayings, he says: "The teaching contains
the sutras and commentaries which were left by the
Buddha and the Bodhisattvas. The Ch'an School, however, only recognizes the masters' sayings. The Buddha's doctrine extends over the eight kinds of supernatural beings in the universe-at-large[20], whereas the
Ch'an masters' sayings are very limited and "adapted to
the level of one kind of people in this country to
guide them in their practice". In the same work The
Origin of Ch'an he writes:

> "Ch'an in Indian language is called **dhyāna**.
> Translated into Chinese, it is the exercise
> of silent meditation which is a general
> appellation for concentration and wisdom.
> The 'origin' means the basic enlightenment of
> the true nature of all beings, also called
> the Buddha nature or mind-ground. Its reali-
> zation is called wisdom and its exercise is
> concentration. The mastery and understanding
> of concentration and wisdom is Ch'an: this
> nature is the original source of Ch'an.
> Therefore one speaks of 'the origin of
> Ch'an', which is also called 'Ch'an truth'
> and 'Ch'an practice'. The original source is
> the truth of Ch'an, the corresponding aban-
> donment of passions is the practice of Ch'an.
> Therefore one talks about truth and practice.
> What is currently being discussed in the
> various schools is often Ch'an theory rather

than practice. Therefore we write about the origin of Ch'an. At this point of time there are people who already consider a glance upon the true nature as Ch'an. They do not catch the meaning of 'truth and practice'."[21]

From Tsung-mi's work it appears first of all that in Hung-chou a Ch'an school had taken root with a strong influence and an original tendency, deriving its authority from Ma-tsu. Tsung-mi himself, who believed that the traditional method of teaching was indissolubly linked with Ch'an Buddhism, could therefore not give his approval to the Hung-chou School. He also pointed to the disadvantages of the unconventional Ch'an teaching, which led to the abuses against which also Lin-chi warned, such as the generalization and the literal interpretation of casual and personal Ch'an statements.

Another source for the history of Ch'an Buddhism in Ma-tsu's time is the Pao-lin chuan. This Ch'an history, already completed in 801, is the work on which all later Ch'an histories are based. It was a product of Ma-tsu's Hung-chou School, and destined to endow the new direction with an official character, by directly linking it with the meanwhile popularized Southern School of Hui-neng. In this work we find the first interpretation of Ch'an history in China which later on became the officially accepted tradition. This could only have happened because of the increasing influence of Ma-tsu's Hung-chou School, which gradually defeated or absorbed all other conflicting versions. Thus the Pao-lin chuan is partially a creation and partially a 'historical' arrangement of many old and new legends about the Indian and Chinese patriarchs and Ch'an

masters, starting with the Seven Buddhas of the Past up
to Ma-tsu inclusively. The report about Ma-tsu's own
'role, however, has been lost; we are therefore dependent on later works which are presumably based on the
Pao-lin chuan.

The earliest and most important of these works is
the Tsu-t'ang chi: "Collection of the Hall of Patriarchs"[22]. This is likewise a collection of biographies
of patriarchs and Ch'an masters, composed in 952, but
soon afterward already lost in China. Recently this
work has been rediscovered in Korea and has been repub-
lished. Although this work disappeared in China, it
remained unchanged throughout the centuries, which
makes, however, its reading more difficult.

Half a century later appeared the Ching-te ch'uan-
teng lu: "Records of the Transmission of the Lamp from
the Ching-te period"[23]. This is a similar collection,
more extensive than the Tsu-t'ang chi, and is considered to be the most significant Ch'an history. Although
the Tsu-t'ang chi had already disappeared when the
Ch'uan-teng lu was composed, they do show a striking
similarity, which suggests that both are based on the
Pao-lin chuan.

In later times many more Ch'an histories have been
written, which one calls 'Histories of the Lamp'.
They all go back to the Pao-lin chuan, of which they
provided supplementary and even 'corrected' versions,
according to the needs of the school which produced the
supplement. In this way a tradition arose which up to
this moment is represented as Ch'an history in Western
literature, but which is mainly based on legends.
According to this traditional version, Ma-tsu would
have been the successor of Nan-yüeh[24] while the latter
would have succeeded Hui-neng, the Sixth Patriarch and

founder of the Southern School which presumably was the basis of all the Ch'an schools surviving the eighth century.

It is, however, well known that this Southern School became only known as such after the appearance of a certain Shen-hui[25] who through his polemical debates and writings had created a controversy between two followers of the fifth patriarch: Shen-hsiu[26] and Hui-neng. The former was at first recognized as the orthodox successor of the fifth patriarch; his school, which especially flourished in the North, was highly respected. Hui-neng was rather unknown and had been active in the South. Shen-hui, however, succeeded in making Hui-neng accepted as the sixth patriarch and himself as the successor of what he called the orthodox 'Southern School'. In this way arose gradually the legendary and popular history of Hui-neng, based on the <u>Platform Scripture of the Sixth Patriarch</u> which had been re-written by Shen-hui[27]. Consequently a rush started of everything which called itself Ch'an to join the ranks of the sixth patriarch and his Southern School. This took place by the end of the eighth century, whereas Hui-neng had already died in 713. Since his disciples had been mostly mountain ascetics, it was rather easy to appeal to one of them in order to create from him a line of succession. This also happened with the Hung-chou School: a certain Nan-yüeh Huai-jang "was exhumed from obscurity" in order to link Ma-tsu with Hui-neng, the sixth patriarch.[28]

According to the traditional version, the Southern School would have been divided after Hui-neng into the line of Nan-yüeh and the line of Ch'ing-yüan[29]. The former would have been Ma-tsu's master and the founder of the Southern School. The Ch'ing-yüan line would have been brought to florescence by Shih-t'ou.[30] In the latter's biography we read: "The Kiangsi master was Ta-chi (Ma-tsu's posthumous title), the Hunan master was Shih-t'ou. One went back and forth between those two, and who had never met these two great masters, was considered as ignorant."[31] This gave rise to the later conception that in Kiangsi and Hunan there were two tendencies and that Shih-t'ou had brought to florescence the Hunan line of Ch'ing-yüan. Since in other sources there is little mention, and in Tsung-mi's work no mention at all of this Ch'ing-yüan line of Shih-t'ou, it is rather doubtful whether it has ever existed. Nan-yüeh, Ch'ing-yüan and their disciples were in fact anonymous 'practitioners of Tao' who led an ascetic life in the mountains. Only in the ninth century their followers made a public appearance, and became known through their numerous praises of the mountain meditation. This type of literature differs fundamentally from the 'Recorded Sayings' of Ma-tsu's Hung-chou School, whose themes are personal encounters and daily events. The polarization between Ma-tsu and Shih-t'ou is therefore considered to be a later interpretation which has been the root cause of numerous historiographic errors.

About Nan-yüeh one only knows that he was a mountain ascetic and a disciple of another follower of the Fifth Patriarch rather than of Hui-neng. What is remarkable in this connection is that Nan-yüeh's biographies mainly relate to Ma-tsu and to the prediction of his coming by Hui-neng[32]. Even the sayings which are traditionally ascribed to Nan-yüeh as being the nucleus of the later Ch'an School, are in fact those of Ma-tsu.[33]

In the historical development of Ch'an before

Ma-tsu the Northern School of Shen-hsiu is of central
importance. Its popularity and influence combined with
the recognition of its orthodox Ch'an teaching, came
much closer to the teaching of the Fifth Patriarch and
Bodhidharma than the simplistic version propagated by
Shen-hsiu. His allegations against the Northern School
even appear to be unjustified. Not only was there no
exclusive practice of the gradual meditation (in contrast with the immediate or sudden method of the Southern School), but enlightenment, which is always immediate was equally of central importance, although the
emphasis on the mastering of meditation was never
absent; this has always been the standpoint of orthodox
Ch'an Buddhism. Moreover, the Northern School did not
limit itself to just the Lankāvatāra sūtra, but deploy-
ed an all-embracing teaching, representing the Yogācāra
as well as the Prajñāpāramitā and the Hua-yen doctrines. Ma-tsu's instructions show a striking similarity with them.

Already in Ma-tsu's time, the legendary version of
the Southern School which made the Sixth Patriarch into
an illiterate who propagated sudden enlightenment
without cultivation, was already fairly influential. A
successor of Hui-neng himself writes about the mislead-
ing propaganda of Shen-hui and his followers: "During
my recent travels I have often encountered this kind
and their success is steadily growing: they number
between 300 and 500. They show contempt for everything
and maintain that this is the essence of the Southern
School. They substitute and falsify the Platform
Scripture; by robbing it from its sacred truth, they
confuse and deceive later followers. How can this be
called the doctrine? It is the end of our Ch'an
School!"[34] According to other sources Shen-hui had

because of his defective understanding, even been rep-
rimanded by Hui-neng in the original Platform Scripture.

The Northern as well as the Southern School,
established in the cities and patronized by the imperial court, lost their vitality by the end of the 8th
century and did not produce any masters of importance.
At that moment, Ma-tsu's Hung-chou School flourished
and was spreading quickly in remote Kiangsi. It received its most powerful expression in Lin-chi, Ma-
tsu's spiritual grandson. He came one generation after
Huang-po and Kui-shan, who operated in Hung-chou, and
established himself far away from there, toward the
North of the Yellow River. It is only since the beginning of the Sung dynasty (960-1279) that Lin-chi and
his school are considered to be the continuation of
Ma-tsu and the Hung-chou School, whereas the Kui-yang
School, the most popular one among the five great Ch'an
schools at the end of the T'ang dynasty (618-907), was
in fact its historic successor. This tradition found
its official certification in the Ssu-chia yü-lu, The
Recorded Sayings of the Four Houses. This work dates
from the beginning of the Sung and represents the four
great masters of 'the golden age of Ch'an Buddhism' as
being one line of succession: Ma-tsu, Pai-chang,
Huang-po and Lin-chi. We shall present part one titled
The Recorded Sayings of Kiangsi Ch'an Master Ma-tsu
Tao-i in translation.

THE RECORDED SAYINGS OF THE CH'AN MASTERS

This literary genre introduced an innovation not to say a revolution into the Buddhist literature. The latter consists of the canonical scriptures of the Tripitaka or 'Three Baskets' and contains the sūtras, or the transmitted discourses of the buddha; the śāstras or commentaries and treatises composed by bodhisattvas and famous teachers; and the vinaya, or the collection of rules and prescriptions. this canon is the only doctrinal authority in Buddhism, and the basis of all Buddhist activity. The extant collection of over two thousand works, varying between a few pages and a few thousands, are translations of or commentaries on the Indian Buddhist Scriptures, which have been partially lost. As the translation process in China continued, original Chinese works, mostly commentaries on sutras, were written since the fifth and sixth centuries and were added to the Canon. From the end of the eighth century, however, a new type of original Chinese texts developed, containing the sayings and anecdotes of the Ch'an masters: they were later also added to the Canon. This type of literature first appeared among the disciples of Ma-tsu.

In the Collection of the Hall of Patriarchs, several times a new phenomenon among Ma-tsu's disciples is mentioned: they started to carefully note down and preserve some sayings and actions of their master. For example, in the biography of Tung-ssu we read: "One continually hears how after Ch'an master Ta-chi (Ma-tsu) had left the world his sayings were written down by people who cherished facts. They were not really able to catch their spirit, and except for the expression: 'the mind is the Buddha', they apparently did

not know a thing about Ma-tsu's teaching. I once
followed our master, but I did not limit myself to
merely following his footsteps..."[35]. Tung-ssu further
criticizes his co-disciples who considered their master's recorded sayings as a precious possession. Also
elsewhere in this collection there is mention of the
recording of sayings attributed to Ma-tsu and transmitted by his followers. Numerous recorded sayings of his
immediate successors have been preserved to the present.[36]

The emergence of this kind of scriptures is connected with the original teaching method first introduced by Ma-tsu. According to Tsung-mi the new insight
of the Hung-chou School centered upon this: "Whatever
one does is a function of the Buddha nature, and that
which speaks and acts is nothing but the Buddha nature.
Ma-tsu indeed says: If you wish to know the mind, then
that which now speaks is your mind, and this mind is
what is called the Buddha, or also True Suchness of the
Buddha in his **Dharma-kaya**, or Tao (the Path). Tao is
not an ideal related to the other side or the here-
after; the very words I now speak are nothing else but
a function of Tao.[37]

Thus Ma-tsu proclaimed in ordinary language and
daily conversation the universal actuality of the
Buddha's truth. He did not restrict himself to the
merely traditional words and concepts about Reality,
but also directly indicated to his monks its instantaneous realization. He addresses himself personally
to those ready for immediate insight, who were also
able to realize it. Especially the lay people among
Ma-tsu's audience would record and present as examples
of awakening those individual sayings and events, which
had been the occasion of a monk's sudden recognition.

When the audiences gathering around such a great teacher as Ma-tsu increased, the occasions for personal
contacts grew fewer and fewer. It is not astonishing
that these recorded sayings and actions were considered
by some to be "the mysterious essence of the teaching",
and "were carefully collected and secretly preserved"
as the sources indicate. That this practice developed
in secret is perhaps due to the Ch'an masters' own
criticism, to begin with Ma-tsu himself who warned his
audience: "do not remember my words!" In Chinese this
could equally mean: "do not record my sayings!" (See
below, section 3).

The texts which originated in the Hung-chou School
did not replace the canonical scriptures. On the
contrary, the sutras were also considered to be recorded sayings of the Buddha, or collections of his very
words. Even the slogan of the later Ch'an school 'we
do not posit texts', was not a rejection of the canonical writings, but signified a return to their vital
essence, which cannot be replaced by any texts. The
success of the new Ch'an method was greatly the outcome
of a new time spirit, in which man as an individual had
been assigned the central focus, together with a general appreciation for the spoken word. Thus the vernacular entered into Chinese Buddhist literature, which up
to then had been rather technical in nature, copied
after the Indian model and only accessible to initi-
ates. The sutras underwent a return to the sources and
were read again as 'living word'. This tendency also
appears from the Histories of the Lamp which have the
manifest intention of illustrating the Buddhist teaching with anecdotes and events from the lives of the
Buddha and the patriarchs.

Gradually notices circulated from which the Recorded <u>Sayings</u> were composed and from which later the **kung-an** were distilled.[38] This does not mean that before Ma-tsu no works had been written about the sayings of certain masters. There already existed the recorded sayings of Bodhidharma and Hung-jen, respectively the First and Fifth Ch'an Patriarchs. Similar works differed from traditional scripture insofar as they emphasized the practice of meditation and the observance of the rules of discipline. Like the <u>Platform</u> <u>Scripture</u> <u>of</u> <u>the</u> <u>Sixth</u> <u>Patriarch</u> and the <u>Recorded</u> <u>Sayings</u> <u>of</u> <u>Shen-hui</u>, they did not contain dialogues and **kung-an** in the sence of Ma-tsu's dialogues (See below, sections 5-33). According to the author of the major **kung-an** collection[39], similar dialogues would have already appeared in India, since they are mentioned in the <u>Histories</u> <u>of</u> <u>the</u> <u>Lamp</u>. He says that the transmission of this teaching is always coupled with similar 'action' but that with the Indian patriarchs one finds a lot of 'theory' and little 'action'. "Yet Mahākāśyapa ordered Ananda to turn over the flagpole, and Nāgārjuna threw a begging bowl in front of Kānadeva; or one showed a circle or one asked questions about a red flag, and so on." These examples, however, derive from Ch'an histories, written after Ma-tsu's time, and are typically Chinese. According to Yanagida Seizan, one may conclude that all Ch'an masters about whom similar anecdotes have been transmitted, belong to Ma-tsu's school, and that their recording started from his time.

The recorded sayings of the Hung-chou School are the main historical source materials with regard to the history of Ch'an Buddhism of that time. It is only since Ma-tsu and with relation to his school, that sufficient material is available to make the mentioning of a relatively clear history at all possible. The

traditional history of Ch'an Buddhism before Ma-tsu is
mainly dependent upon later legends.[40]

The subsequent history of the recorded sayings of
the Chinese Ch'an masters is characterized by a contin-
uous development. Their original statements have been
received in a literary form which itself evolved,
causing them often to be transformed. Commentaries by
later Ch'an masters on these sayings and actions were
equally considered to be essential and were included in
the Canon. By the end of the T'ang dynasty a movement
arose, especially in the Fa-yen school, which edited
anew all previously recorded sayings. The definitive
texts such as they are known to us today, are the work
of the Huang-lung School, which succeeded the Fa-yen
School. This branch of the Lin-chi line was one of the
five Ch'an schools at the end of T'ang and was located
on Mount Lu. Its activity signified the starting point
of a new evolution in Ch'an Buddhism, which resulted
into the **kung-an** literature of the Sung period.

The recorded sayings of the Hung-chou School, in
spite of their fast spread and their great popularity,
were not immediately recognized by other schools of
Buddhism. It was mainly the Huang-lung School and the
publication of the Ssu-chia yü-lu which must receive
credit for providing Ma-tsu's Ch'an Buddhism with an
orthodox and official statute. Since this work originated at the same time as Ma-tsu's school and in close
connection with him, it is also titled the Ma-tsu
ssu-chia lu or Records of the Four Houses of Ma-tsu.[41]

THE TEXT

1. Biography (Section 1)

The early Ch'an school in China only counted a small number of followers. Bodhidharma, the First Ch'an Patriarch, did not appoint more than one successor whom he entrusted with the authentic continuation of the Ch'an teaching. With the Fifth Patriarch, the Ch'an school took flight: it spread more widely and its succession was not any longer committed to one man. Although according to the traditional Ch'an history, Hui-neng was the Sixth and last Patriarch or direct successor of Bodhidharma, there are among the Tun-huang manuscripts historical documents which mention eleven successors of the Fifth Patriarch. They ante-date Shen-hui and the polarization between the Northern and Southern Schools, out of which appeared Hui-neng as the Sixth Patriarch, and they thus contradict the traditional version.

Even Ma-tsu's earliest biographies[42] have been influenced by the tendency which connects all Ch'an schools with the Southern School of Hui-neng. They talk about Nan-yüeh Huai-jang, who on Mount Nan-yüeh transmitted the teaching of the Sixth Patriarch and whom Ma-tsu after his ordination went to visit. According to Tsung-mi, Ma-tsu after the death of his master Ch'u-chi (648-734) became a wandering monk, who, following the general custom, practiced meditation wherever he went and accidentally met Nan-yüeh. His master Ch'u-chi was the successor of Chih-hsien (609-702), who was one of the eleven successors of the Fifth Patriarch. Ma-tsu belonged to one of the two lines started by Chih-hsien, viz. that of the Ching-chung monastery in Chengtu (Szuchuan province). We do not

know much more about Ma-tsu's origin and training,
since his biographies mostly consist of later additions
concerning his encounter with Nan-yüeh and his prediction by Hui-neng, as is also the case in this biography.

The words with which Nan-yüeh instructs Ma-tsu and
points to the true nature of practice and realization
show a striking similarity to the texts of the Southern
School. We read, for instance, in Hui-neng's biography: "All Ch'an masters in the (Northern) capital
say that one should sit in **dhyāna** and practice concentration, if one wants to acquire an understanding of
Tao; there has never been anyone who was liberated,
except through **dhyānas** and **samādhis**...". The master
answered: "One realizes Tao through the mind; how does
it have anything to do with sitting?"[43]

In the works of Shen-hui, one encounters numerous
similar statements, and reference is made to the following passage from the <u>Vimalakīrti-nirdeśa</u>:

> ...once, as I was sitting in meditation under
> a tree in a grove, Vimalakīrti came and said:
> Śāriputra, meditation is not necessarily
> sitting. For meditation means the nonappear-
> ance of body and mind in the three worlds (of
> desire, form and no form); giving no thought
> to inactivity when in nirvāna while appearing
> (in the world) with respect-inspiring deport-
> ment; not straying from the Truth while at-
> tending to worldly affairs; the mind abiding
> neither within nor without; being imperturb-
> able to wrong views during the practice of
> the thirty-seven contributory stages leading
> to enlightenment; and not wiping out troubles
> (kleśa) while entering the state of nirvāna.

If you can thus sit in meditation, you   will win the Buddha's seal.[44]

The arguments which Nan-yüeh adduces are   inspired by the Diamond sūtra, which was also the basis for Shen-hui's interpretation of Ch'an Buddhism. One knows that the so-called preference of the Ch'an patriarchs for this sutra above all others is a creation of his. For Ma-tsu, the Diamond sūtra has no importance; his own words show little similarity to the teaching method of his so-called master, which is clearly based on this sutra and its terminology. The theme which governs the whole dialogue between Ma-tsu and Nan-yüeh, the rela- tivity of everything that has characteristics, is also very central in the Diamond sūtra: "Wherever there are characteristics, there is illusion. If one sees   char- acteristics as non-characteristics, one sees the Tathā- gata."[45] Together with 'empty' and 'non-abiding', 'without characteristics' constitutes the triple dharma-seal, which is the seal of Buddha-truth, expres- sing its authentic transmission.

According to later versions of Hui-neng's biogra- phy he became awakened upon hearing a sentence from the Diamond sūtra: "You must develop a mind abiding no- where". Striking is the similarity with Ma-tsu's 'con- version': "With respect to the dharmas which abide nowhere, you must not grasp or reject anything...". The renouncing of all duality between what is consider- ed good and wanted for oneself and what is considered bad and rejected, is also proposed by Hui-neng: "When with respect to the dharmas you do not grasp nor reject anything, then you see your nature and perfect the Buddha path". This classical theme will return with Ma-tsu and all other Ch'an masters.

The 'doctrine of the mind-ground' is a fundamental

teaching method in Buddhism, which directly points at
the mind; it enjoyed privileged status in the Ch'an
school. The mind is as the ground, and as from the
earth all life arises, so also in the mind everything
appears: it is the back-ground from which thought and
consequently the world of diversity arise and into
which they disappear again. According to the Pao-lin
chuan and the subsequent Ch'an histories, the 'essential doctrine of the mind' would have been transmitted
by each Buddha and Patriarch to his successor by means
of a stanza of which the mind-ground was the central
theme. In the Platform Scripture, Hui-neng cites the
stanzas of his predecessors and thus confirms his
orthodox succession. He also states that after him the
mind doctrine will no longer be personally transmitted,
but that these stanzas are sufficient to warrant the
authentic Ch'an doctrine. His own stanza is as follows:

> The mind-ground contains the seed of living
> things,
> When the rain of the Dharma falls the flowers
> are brought forth.
> When you yourself have awakened to the living
> seeds of the flower[?],
> The fruit of enlightenment matures of it-
> self.[46]

It is believed that Hui-neng through this stanza
would have appointed Nan-yüeh as his successor, and
thereupon would have announced the advent of Ma-tsu.
"The sermon that I have just preached, is like the rain
that waters the great earth, and your Buddha natures
are like the many seeds that sprout when they encounter
the wetness."[47] In this biography Ma-tsu is being appointed as Nan-yüeh's successor in an almost identical

manner, and in this way connected with Hui-neng as the orthodox successor of the patriarchs. In turn he will summarize the Ch'an teaching in a stanza about the mind-ground.[48]

According to other Ch'an histories, Ma-tsu was not the only successor of Nan-yüeh: "The master had in total six disciples who 'entered his room'. To each of them he gave the 'seal of approval', in these words:

All six of you have together been witnesses of my body, and to each one part of it will be allotted. One has deserved my eyebrows for he excels through his impressive attitude (Ch'ang-hao). One has deserved my eyes, for he excels through his staring gaze (Chih-ta). One has deserved my ears, for he excels in the listening to the instruction (T'an-jan). One has deserved my nose for he excels in breathing technique (Shen-chao). One has deserved my tongue, for he excels in speaking (Yen-chün). One has deserved my mind, for he excels in the old and the new (Tao-i)."[49]

The expressions 'to enter the room' and 'to receive the seal of approval' signify that a disciple is recognized as an authentic successor by his master and in this way is entrusted 'secretly with the mind-seal'. This happens secretly, not that anything is kept hidden for non-initiates, but because it has to do with a 'spiritual' transmission. This transmission has been described by Hui-neng as 'through the mind to transmit the mind' and by Shen-hui: "The inner transmission happens through the mind-seal: the seal is identical with the original mind".[50] When the master impresses his 'seal' in the mind of the disciple, there exists identity between both. The disciple is the master's 'off-print'. "To stamp the mind with the mind, so that there is no longer any difference between mind and mind", Huang-po says.[51] The disciple is not only recognized as 'stamped' as a successor, but, moreover, there is an absolute identity, which guarantees or 'seals' the pure transmission of the teaching. 'The seal of approval' and to give or to receive 'the seal-proof' are still current today. Although the practice of 'secretly entering the room' has been opposed by the Lin-chi (Rinzai) school, it has yet remained in existence in present-day Japan.

Concerning Ma-tsu's last recorded saying: "during the day in the presence of the Buddha; at night in the presence of the Buddha", many commentaries have been written. This expression pronounced shortly before his death, may also mean: "Sun-face Buddha, Moon-face Buddha". In the Sutra of Buddha-names, these two names occur: "A Sun-face Buddha lives in the world for 1800 years; a Moon-face Buddha only lives a day and a night". This religious interpretation does not differ essentially from the deeper meaning which Ma-tsu's statement also has, namely the permanence within impermanence, the absolute consciousness within the relative phenomena of time and space, life and death. One Buddha appears for 1800 years; another just for a moment, but in their Buddha-nature nothing changes. Another translation: "During the day time I have a Buddha-face; at night I have a Buddha-face", has this commentary: "The master does not show the least facial change, whether it is day or night, whether the four elements (the body) are in harmony or not."[52] Ma-tsu's last saying may perhaps be considered to be the summary of his message, which is also the message of Ch'an Buddhism: the Buddha is the Living Presence.

2. Instructions (Sections 2-4)

"Ma-tsu's first instruction is a direct exposition of the mind-doctrine transmitted by Bodhidharma of the Ch'an school based on the words of the Buddha which summarize the Lankāvatāra sūtra: 'The Buddha's proclamation has the mind as its essence and the no-method as its teaching method'. In this context 'Mind' is not the mind of the psychic consciousness. The expression 'mind' or 'nature' is the Chinese term which points to the absolute potentiality and activity of the transcendent-and-immanent totality. With the teaching method (literally 'gate' or 'entrance') of 'no-method' is meant the entrance to the dharma which does not use any form or definite method as 'temporary means of salvation'. In this instruction, Ma-tsu summarizes the Buddha's teaching, especially by refuting the nature of matter as real, while revealing the emptiness of the original substance of self-nature, the one origin of mind and matter. Although incessantly creative, enlightened nature is by itself in substance and function always empty, clear and pure."[53]

Bodhidharma transmitted to the Second Ch'an Patriarch the Lankāvatāra sūtra with these words: "This is the teaching of the mind-ground of the Tathāgata, through which all sentient beings may become enlightened. I left South-India for this Eastern land because people in China have the capacity for the Great Vehicle (Mahāyāna)." Ma-tsu explicitly bases his teaching on the original Ch'an Buddhism of Bodhidharma and the

Lankāvatāra sūtra[54]. With this sutra is connected the 'consciousness-only' doctrine of the Yogācāra-school of Mahāyāna Buddhism, which manifests the tendency of revaluating the religious attitude and practice of original Buddhism. The most important work of this school is Asanga's Yogācārabhūmi-śāstra[55], which thoroughly explains the real process of practice and realization. This work, together with the Mahāprajñāpāramitā-śāstra[56], attributed to Nāgārjuna, has become the fundamental diptych of Buddhist interpretation. The latter work belongs to the Prajñā- (or wisdom) literature of Mādhyamika philosophy, also called 'new wisdom school'. This direction is a rather theorizing and intellectualizing tendency in Mahāyāna, whereas the Yogācāra is more directed toward practice and realization.

The best known sutra of the wisdom literature is the Diamond sūtra[57] which became very popular within the Southern Ch'an school. It is a fundamental introduction in which 'insight' is explained. The Lankāvatāra sūtra which discusses the further practice and mystical realization, occupied a central position in the Northern Ch'an school, which comes closer to the original Ch'an and the Yogācāra direction.

The quote "The Buddha's proclamation has mind as its essence and no-method as its teaching method" is not specifically found in this sutra. One can, however, find in it such expressions as: "the Buddha's proclamation is the mind"; "the three worlds are merely expressions of the mind"; "everything is a phenomenon of one's mind"; "the non-instruction is the instruction of the Buddha": these are the themes which have been elaborated upon by Ma-tsu in this instruction.

He further frequently cites the Vimalakīrti-nir-

deśa[58] without quoting its title. This is probably due
to the fact that this text, related to the wisdom—literature, was extremely well known in all schools of
Chinese Buddhism, and even exerted a remarkable influence on the total cultural patrimony of China.   A
commonplace was for instance Ma—tsu's quotation:
"Whoever seeks the Dharma, should not seek anything".
These are the last words from Vimalakīrti's discourse
about 'seeking the Dharma':

> The Dharma is (absolute and) immaculate, but
> if you are defiled by (the thought of) Dharma
> and even that of nirvana, this is pollution
> which runs counter to the quest of Dharma.
> Dharma cannot be practised and if it is put
> into practice, this implies something (i.e.
> an object) to be practised and is not the
> quest of Dharma.   Dharma is beyond grasping
> and rejecting, and if you grasp or reject it,
> this is grasping or rejecting (something
> else) but not the quest of Dharma.   Dharma is
> beyond position but if you give it a place,
> this is clinging to space but not the quest
> of Dharma.   Dharma is formless but if you
> rely on form to conceive the Dharma, this is
> search for form but not the quest of Dharma.
> Dharma is not an abode but if you want to
> stay in it this is dwelling in (an objective)
> Dharma, but not the quest of (absolute)
> Dharma.   Dharma can be neither seen, nor
> heard nor felt nor known but if you want to
> see, hear, feel and know it, this is the
> functioning of your (discriminatory) seeing,
> hearing, feeling and knowing but not the
> quest of Dharma.   Dharma is (transcendental-

ly) inactive (wu wei) but if you are set on
worldly activities, this is a search for the
worldly way of life but not the quest of
Dharma. Therefore, Śāriputra, the quest of
Dharma does not imply seeking anything whatsoever.[59]

The Vimalakīrti-nirdeśa, a literary masterpiece, found
itself wonderfully attuned to the Chinese mentality.
Especially passages about Śāriputra's meditation, Vimalakīrti's silence and liberation through sin, were
popular. Concerning this last theme, also broached by
Ma-tsu, Vimalakīrti says:

. . . sin is not to be apprehended within, or
without, or between the two. Why? The
Buddha has said, 'Living beings are afflicted
by the passions of thought, and they are
purified by the purification of thought.'

'Reverend Upāli, the mind is neither
within nor without, nor is it to be apprehended between the two. Sin is just the same
as the mind, and all things are just the same
as sin. They do not escape this same reality.'

'Reverend Upāli, this nature of the
mind, by virtue of which your mind, reverend,
is liberated--does it ever become afflicted?'

'Never,' I replied.

'Reverend Upāli, the minds of all living
beings have that very nature. Reverend
Upāli, passions consist of conceptualizations. The ultimate non-existence of these
conceptualizations and imaginary fabrica-
tions--that is the purity that is the intrinsic nature of the mind. Misapprehensions are

passions. The ultimate absence of misapprehensions is the intrinsic nature of the mind.
The presumption of self is passion. The
absence of self is the intrinsic nature of
the mind. Reverend Upāli, all things are
without production, destruction and duration,
like magical illusions, clouds, and light-
ning; all things are evanescent, not remaining even for an instant; all things are like
dreams, hallucinations, and unreal visions;
all things are like the reflection of the
moon in water and like a mirror-image; they
are born of mental construction.[60],
Herewith is announced a central theme of this text,
which we also find in Ma-tsu and all Ch'an masters.
"Do not think (in terms of) good and evil. What at
this moment is your original face from before your
birth. . ." is a legendary statement of Hui-neng, which
in later Ch'an training became an important kung-an.
"To reject error and to grasp the truth is artificial
and false because of the mental attitude of grasping
and rejecting," we read in Yung-chia. And Lin-chi:
"The sages turn away from the profane and find joy in
th sacred. They have not yet forgotten the grasping
and rejecting, for them there still are defiled and
pure thoughts. This, however, does not at all tally
with the understanding of the Ch'an school."

Good and evil, pure and impure (sacred and profane, right and wrong, pro and contra, etc., see Section 4), are not reality but perceptions of reality.
It is the thinking which proceeds from a 'self', that
distinguishes 'objects', conceives of these objects as
wholesome or unwholesome, and appropriates the good
while rejecting the evil. "Enlightenment does not know

either grasping or rejecting. Enlightenment is non-duality; it does not know either thoughts or objects of thoughts."[61]

'Phenomenon and principle' (see p. 85) are concepts introduced by Hua-yen philosophy as synonymous of form (rūpa) and emptiness (śūnyatā), since these terms in Chinese have a concrete meaning, namely colour or material appearance and empty space or absence of objects. This pair of concepts (literally: event or fact, and principle or truth, also translated as appearance and reality) occurs in Ch'an literature more frequently as substance and function. Appearance is function, operation or manifestation of reality; reality is the substance of what appears.[62] This theme is related to the Mādhyamika doctrine of the identity between samsāra and nirvāna:

> Noumenon and Phenomena are not two separate
> sets of entities, nor are they two states of
> the same thing. The absolute is the only
> real; it is the reality of samsāra, which is
> sustained by false construction (kalpanā).
> The absolute looked at through the thought-
> forms of constructive imagination is the
> empirical world; and conversely, the absolute
> is the world viewed sub specie aeternitatis,
> without these distorting media of thought.[63]

The non-obstruction of phenomenon and principle is a central theme in Hua-yen doctrine, which is based on the Hua-yen sūtra[64], 'king of the Mahāyāna sutras'. According to the Chinese tradition it was the first discourse made by the Buddha: immediately after his enlightenment, he propounded his deepest doctrine, the teaching of Totality[65]. In Ma-tsu's time, the Hua-yen doctrine still exercised a major influence, and thus he refers to concepts as 'non-obstruction', unity and plurality, etc. The Hua-yen doctrine occupied a prestigious position in the Northern School and received later on much attention in the Ts'ao-tung and Lin-chi Schools as well.[66]

Ma-tsu's first instruction is a classical summary of some central themes in Buddhist doctrine, as analyzed in the Chinese Yogācāra (consciousness-only) and Hua-yen philosophies. The original Ch'an teaching had therefore little of a mysterious, legendary 'other outside the teaching', as was later under the influence of the Southern School often stated.

By way of illustration we cite a contemporary statement, which, because of its modern, non-Buddhist terminology, is able to make the universal mind-doctrine of Ch'an Buddhism more accessible and intelligible; moreover its ideas show a striking similarity to the teaching of Ma-tsu:

> When it becomes thoroughly clear to us that each observed phenomenon--feeling, thought, sense observation or situation--is totally dependent on the presence of an observing something, of an observer, then our point of gravity is spontaneously and effortlessly shifted toward a location outside the observed; in other words, we then find ourselves at a distance from that 'object'. And if afterward it becomes clear that the observed is something like an action of the observing or the observer, the essential understanding becomes possible. This discovery, this acknowledgment takes us along toward the conscious, lived Experience, which this in-ground is. We know ourselves then

only to be this in-ground; we are only this
background, just as is the case between two
concepts or two observations: the first one
has disappeared, the second one is not yet
there, and at that 'moment' there only is
that background. Precisely the same happens
when a desire is totally fulfilled.

This proto-ground is our true nature,
which is completely free of everything that
is time and space. It is the presence of
this proto-experience which enables the
efflorescence of time and space, but time and
space do not leave in it a single trace and
do not influence it in any manner—just as a
mirror does not change.

In this Experience it appears that the
world which we used to consider as an objective reality and in which we participate with
our physicality, our thinking and feeling, is
an expression of this basic nature, which
does not know 'outer' or 'inner'; world-and-
I; God-and-I. The other-than-I-myself is as
if it were evaporated in the Experience,
which exactly therefore is not an experience
in the current meaning; there exists no
longer somebody experiencing something outside himself. What we experience in our
basic nature, is perfect completion, it is
the ultimate and highest satisfaction, which
cannot be diminished or complemented by
anything.

Nothing can be reached, there is nothing
that can be appropriated, sought or found.
The satisfaction which we try to find with

all possible means and with much struggle, is
the closest to us, much nearer than any feeling or thought. This proto-nature has never
been created, nor did it ever begin; it did
not arise in order to disappear once again.[67]

"The second instruction (Section 3, pp.
80-82) starts from the Buddha's teaching
about the modes of existence, arising and
ceasing, of body and mind: they are merely
functions and appearances which arise from
the mind-nature. They do not offer any
support and are non-existing illusions as
'flowers in the sky'. The self-nature which
has the ability to cause arising and ceasing
is originally still, empty and pure. Whoever
does not understand the reality of this one
truth is an 'ordinary (unenlightened) person'. Whoever realizes this transcendent
self-nature, which goes beyond concrete
reality, has reached the holy state of liberation. The level, however, of enlightenment
may be deep or superficial, thorough or
imperfect. Superficial and imperfect realization is the fruit of the Small Vehicle:
the śrāvaka- and pratyeka-buddha levels of
arhatship. Whoever is profoundly and thoroughly enlightened, is a great bodhisattva
who becomes a Buddha through ultimate enlightenment. Yet, no matter which stage is
reached in the process of transformation of
practice and realization, from ordinary
person to Buddhahood, it is never outside the
self-nature of the original mind, which all

sentient beings have in common with the Buddha."[68]

In this instruction Ma-tsu often returns to 'false thinking': 'the mind-content' of the 'ordinary man', the 'origin of life and death in the three worlds'. Man is originally enlightened; his not being enlighten- ed is only accidental and not intrinsic. What alien- ates him from his own being is false thinking. Since, however, he is not conscious of this alienation, he is unable to conceptualize the origin and nature of this false thinking. Its root is 'ignorance', the state of error which precedes all other states of alienation. Ignorance and not the self is the most fundamental problem in Buddhism, just as original sin or proto- error in Christianity precedes individual existence. "The original error is not an error of the self, but an error which brought the world and the self into exis- tence. This error is the ignorance through which sepa- ration arises, namely a world with 'selves' who con- sider themselves as separate. The appearance of the self generates the world, its ceasing makes it dis- appear. Beyond the self and the world, there is the eternal 'I am', immutable and without cause. What ignorance has added to the 'I am', i.e. the self and the world, is removed through knowledge. What then remains is our true nature."[69]

The mind-contents of the ordinary man are false thoughts; he takes for real conceptions which are opposed to reality. False or erroneous representations are all mental functions which are projected upon the experience of reality. It is the thinking which is attached to its own contents beyond reality; the basic neurosis which arises from a self-and-objects and main- tains this duality. "False thinking envelops itself in

the way a silkworm forms itself into a cocoon." It is
the basic delusion which mentally discriminates all
phenomena as 'things'. "In the ordinary man's consciousness, which errs about reality, dharmas and characters arise. He attaches himself to characters and
maintains ideas about them; on the basis of these
ideas, he appropriates himself qualities, which are not
real. . . . All beings are from eternity subject to
life and death, succeeding each other without interrup-
tion. This is because they do not know the ever-pres-
ent, true mind, whose substance is naturally pure and
shining. They foster false conceptions. These
thoughts are not true. Therefore there is samsāra."
Thus the Śūrangama-sūtra[70], from which many expressions
in this instruction are derived.

This sutra is perhaps the most cherished among the
Buddhist works in China. The first few chapters deal
with insight and the immediate enlightenment; the
remaining chapters with gradual realization, which is
being analyzed openly and clearly into all its implications. We cite here only a short passage concerning
the erroneous disposition of the śrāvaka, against which
also Ma-tsu warns in the same terms:

> Instead of remembering in a worldly manner
> characters conditioned through 'the hearing
> of a voice' (śrāvaka is translated in Chinese
> as 'voice-hearer') you would do better to
> reflect inwardly upon the original nature of
> hearing. . . . On the basis of sound, words
> and concepts exist which constitute the Bud-
> dha's instruction. . . . As soon as one
> sense-faculty (hearing) returns to the
> source, all six faculties are liberated.

This instruction further reminds us of the Lotus
sūtra[71] in which the śrāvaka is described as one who
rejoices in the Small Vehicle. Thus five thousand
followers refuse to listen to the Buddha's 'higher' or
Mahāyāna teaching. They prefer to remain unilaterally
in emptiness. The sutra further speaks about 'burnt
shoots which cannot grow any more"; the realization of
the śrāvaka is called an 'illusion' and the arhat's
enlightenment 'imperfect nirvāna'. The Lotus sūtra,
one of the earliest and most famous of all Mahāyāna
texts, emphasizes the doctrine that there is only one
path to Buddhahood, which is not limited to time and
space, but is universal and open to all.

> "The third instruction (Section 4, pp. 83-86)
> is a practical application of the doctrine
> explained in the Mahāyāna śāstra: The Awak-
> ening of Faith: arising and ceasing are
> functions of the one mind; the true reality
> of the self-nature is originally nirvāna
> which does neither arise nor cease. The
> ultimate consequences of practice and action
> which in an honest and total realization of
> the Path are presupposed, are pointed out.
> Whoever applies himself to it, must thor-
> oughly penetrate if he wants to understand,
> and must be really awakened if he wants to be
> enlightened."[72]

The Awakening of Faith, a condensed summary of
Mahāyāna doctrine, exercised a strong influence on
various Buddhist schools, especially on the Hua-yen
school. It also enjoyed high prestige in the Northern
Ch'an School, in which it constituted an integral part
of its teaching. Its influence is equally noticeable

with Ma-tsu as well as in the Ch'an schools after him.

A key-word in the śāstra is 'Tathāgata-womb'. Ultimate Reality is called the **Dharma-kāya** ('Body' of Essence) which in its various aspects is also described as **Dharma-dhātu** ('Dharma-realm') and **Tathāgata-garbha** ('Tathāgata-womb'). As the terms mind and original nature are also expressions for the Absolute involved in the sphere of relative existence, so is the worldly condition expressed in terms of Tathāgata-womb. 'Tathāgata', which originally is a title of the historical Buddha Śākyamuni, points toward the eternal, essential Buddha, who is in germ or embryonically present as if it were in a womb or uterus. It is the Buddha-nature which is intrinsically but latently present in human nature waiting to be actualized; or absolute consciousness, subject to the errors and frustrations of the world. Absolute Reality, as unmanifest but truly present, is called the 'Dharma-body', namely the essential and spiritual (mystical) 'body' of the Buddha. A Buddha is the embodiment of the Dharma (the Absolute Truth), which is the true Reality ('Body' or **kāya**) of each historical Buddha. This 'Body' is 'invisible and omnipresent, imperishable and perfectly pure, undifferentiated and universal . . . All beings live, move and exist in it'. This is the essential Buddhahood in which all Buddhas are united and to which all beings are destined. It stretches all over the Dharma-realm, which is the world in its fundamental meaning, the totality of all world-systems and all possible world-systems, the 'universum' as it appears to someone who realizes the Dharma. The Dharma-world is the 'ground', the origin and essence of all that exists. Earthly reality is the Dharma-realm in its spatio-temporal aspect. Human existence is the incarnation of the eternal as Tathāgata womb.

"In these three instructions, the central theme is from the beginning clearly set out: 'the Buddha's proclamation has the mind as its essence and the no-method as its teaching method'. Toward the end, the consequences of true understanding and real awakening are pointed out: they ultimately result in non-practice and non-realization. This does not at all mean that Ch'an Buddhism does not put emphasis upon practice and life attitude, realization and enlightenment. It only signifies that when practice and realization have reached the authentic and ultimate result, there is no further need for practice and realization. It is then a spontaneous revelation, a natural presence. It is as with someone who learns a trade, an art or a science: when he has reached the highest degree of achievement, he has become one with his trade. The same applies when practice has realized the highest level; then the essence of the Tathāgata, the supreme wisdom, is simply and spontaneously present and will be always and every-where with you--Such is the Great Nirvāna."[73]

3. Dialogues (Sections 5-33, pp. 87-102)

The Recorded Sayings of the Ch'an masters are in the first place collections of their statements about 'reality' (or 'principle'), namely theoretical dissertations which are most often, as in the case of Ma-tsu's instructions, addressed to a community of Ch'an monks. Besides these they contain dialogues and **kung-an** which narrate 'events' from the masters' lives. These are reports of individual conversations or happenings which have been of crucial significance in the learning process of the Ch'an monks. These testimonies are mostly limited to momentary glimpses, in which the doctrinal context and the concrete aspects of practice and realization, to which they actually allude, are not mentioned. Where the information about factual situations in which the dialogues took place is missing, they are naturally often hard to understand. The typical Ch'an stories presuppose therefore insight into the background in which they appear. "The **kung-an** can only be used by persons with an enlightened mind who wish to verify their insight", says Ch'an master Chung-feng of the Lin-chi school, in which the **kung-an** method was developed.

The popular Ch'an stories are not at all meant as a method of instruction, which could replace the Buddhist teaching and practice. They should rather be read as a scenario in which more advanced Buddhists appear on the stage. For illustration we present here a free interpretation of a dialogue between Ma-tsu and Shih-chiu (section 18, p. 94). It gives a striking example of the very appropriate and direct **kung-an** style, which is probably hard to understand upon first reading.

Shih-chiu, a follower of Master Wu-chiu, visits

the famous Ma-tsu to test his own insight. Ma-tsu asks: 'What has Wu-chiu lately been discussing?' Shih-chiu says: 'Many people do not quite know what it is all about'. (He does not say what he has grasped as Ma-tsu's question was asking for, but says it in other words: we are all well set on the path, we cannot make it quite to the finishing line, no matter how Wu-chiu explains. Ma-tsu, however, notices that he has not learned in vain and asks him to say something about enlightenment:) 'Let us not consider the ignorance of others. What do you yourself think of that quiet, secret sentence?' (or let me hear something quietly, or whisper something into my ear, about the spiritual transmission). Thereupon Chiu stands up and advances three steps. (That means that he is enlightened, and as soon as Ma-tsu sees that he has the correct insight, he says, without waiting for Chiu's answer, which could have been a box on the ear as well as a statement:) 'I have seven canings for you and your master. Is it with your full conviction?' (He wants to test him with beatings. According to Lin-chi, beatings are sometimes meant as a punishment, sometimes as a reward). Chiu says: 'If you take them first, I shall have them next.' (He believes that both of them deserve a beating, in other words that Ma-tsu as well as Wu-chiu and he himself have the correct insight.)

Another typical conversation is the one with Wu-yeh (Section 15, p. 92), a representation of the conventional teaching method. The Sung kao-seng chuan offers a more extensive version of this encounter, which is based on the historically reliable memorial of Wu-yeh himself.[74] This version, moreover, gives insight in the origin and significance of the kung-an literature: for a bridge is made here between the

recorded sayings, which at first collected the historical teaching, and the later **kung-an** literature which
was restricted to the most striking events and utter-
ances of the earlier Ch'an masters, which were frequently modified and are therefore not too reliable as
historical source materials. "Ch'an master Wuyeh of
Fen-chou came to study with Ma-tsu. Once Ma-tsu observed his elegant appearance and his voice sounding as
a bell. Thereupon he said: 'What an impressive
Buddha-hall, too bad there is no Buddha in it'. Yeh
fell on his knees and asked: 'The scripture of the
Three Vehicles I understand in its general outline. I
continuously hear about the Ch'an principle: "the mind
is the Buddha", but I cannot really understand it'.
Ma-tsu said: 'Precisely the mind which cannot understand it, that is it, and further there is nothing
else. When you do not understand, it is error. If you
do understand, it is enlightenment. If you err, you
are a living being. If you are enlightened, you are a
Buddha. The Path is not separate from living beings.
How would there be a Buddha outside them? It is as
with a hand which makes a fist, while the fist totally
remains a hand'. During these words Yeh was suddenly
enlightened. He started crying and said to Ma-tsu:
'It has always been maintained that the Buddha-path is
long and far, and that it can only be realized after a
great number of kalpas of effort and suffering. Today
I know for the first time that the true reality of the
Dharma-kāya is actually perfectly present in myself.
All dharmas arise from the mind; they are only ideas
and shapes and not reality.' Thereupon Ma-tsu said:
'So is it, so is it. The nature of all dharmas does
neither arise nor cease. All dharmas are fundamentally
empty and quiet. In the scriptures is said: all

dharmas are originally and always appearances of nirvāna; or: the dwelling-place of ultimate emptiness; or
again: all dharmas have emptiness as their seat.[75]
That is precisely the place which is nowhere, where the
Buddhas and Tathāgatas are. When you know this, you
are in the dwelling-place of emptiness, sitting on the
chair of the empty Dharma. Whether you lift your feet
or put them down, you do not leave the place of enlightenment. Understanding is instantaneous, and
further there is nothing gradual. This is what is
called to climb the mountain of nirvāna without moving
one's feet."

NOTES TO (NAN HUAI-CHIN'S) PREFACE
(by Bavo Lievens)

1. Hu Shih: "Chinese Zennism arose not out of Indian yoga or dhyāna but as a revolt against it". ("Development of Zen Buddhism in China", in The Chinese Social and Political Science Review, vol. 15, no. 4, p. 483).

2. Besides the Ch'an school, there were the Lü-tsung, the Chü-she, the Ch'eng-shih, the San-lun, the T'ien-t'ai, the Hua-yen, the Fa-hsiang, the Mi-tsung, and the Ching-t'u schools.

3. The disparate doctrinal statements of the Hīnayāna and the Mahāyāna had been harmonized in China according to an ingenious structure by which several levels and periods of teaching in the Buddha's life were distinguished. See for example L. Hurvitz, Chih-I (538-597). An Introduction to The Life and Ideas of a Chinese Buddhist Monk. Brussels, Mélanges Chinois et Bouddhiques, vol. 12, 1962.

4. The term 'school' (tsung) indicates a specific direction in Buddhism, which stresses a particular but essential aspect of Buddhist teaching or practice, whereas, 'teaching' (chiao, doctrine, instruction) is the totality of all classical Buddhist doctrinal tenets. Each school approximates via its own method of teaching and practice, the universal truth, which through purely theoretical knowledge of the doctrine cannot be realized. The same applies the other way around: the unilateral practice of a particular school or sect without insight into the whole of the Buddha's message, cannot lead up to total realization.

5. Yung-Chia, Song of Enlightenment (Cheng Tao Ke), (T.2014, vol. 48, p. 369a) translated by Lu K'uan-yu or Charles Luk, Ch'an and Zen Teaching, third series, (London: Rider, 1962), pp. 116-145.

6. The body of Buddhist Scriptures consists of three parts: (i) the sūtras, or the transmitted sermons of the Buddha; (ii) the vinaya, or the collection of the rules of discipline; and (iii) the abhidharma and śāstras, or the collected commentaries and treatises by great Buddhist scholars.

7. "The four dhyānas and eight samādhis" are a technical expression to describe the meditation process.

8. "Dhyāna of the Tathāgata" means the classical meditation practice of the historical Buddha, whereas "dhyāna of the patriarchs" refers to the teaching and practice of meditation taught in China by Bodhidharma, the Indian founder of Ch'an Buddhism, and by his successors.

9. The main Hīnayāna texts followed in the practice of meditation are:
    Ta an-pan shou-i ching (T. 602, vol. 15);
    Ch'an-hsing san-shih-ch'i p'in ching (T. 604);
    Ch'an-hsing fa-hsiang ching (T. 605);
    Hsiu-hsing tao-ti ching (T. 606);
    Tao-ti ching (T. 607);
    Ch'an-yao ching (T. 609);
    Nei-shen-kuan chang-chu ching (T. 610);
    Fa-kuan ching (T. 611);
    Shen-kuan ching (T. 612);
    Ch'an-mi yao-fa ching (T. 613);
    Tso-ch'an san-mei ching (T. 614);
    Ch'an-fa yao-chieh (T. 616);
    Ssu-wei lüeh-yao fa (T. 617);

Ta-mo-to-lo ch'an ching (T. 618);

Fo-yin san-mei ching (T. 621);

Ju-lai tu-cheng tzu-shih san-mei ching (T. 623).

10. Ssu-Fen lü (T. 1428, vol. 22).

11. Fan-wang ching (T. 1484, vol. 24).

12. Yü-ch'ieh-shih ti lun (T. 1579, vol. 30).

13. Chin-kang ching (T. 235, vol. 8).

14. Leng-ch'ieh ching.

15. Wei-mo ching.

16. Nieh-p'an ching (T. 374, vol. 12) translated by K. Yamamoto.

17. Miao-fa lien-hua ching.

18. Fa-hsiang.

19. Yü-lu (Japanese: goroku).

20. Literally 'public case'.

21. See p. 56 for 'reality' and 'events'.

NOTES TO THE INTRODUCTION

1. In Western literature, one encounters both opin-
    ions: that Ch'an is the rejection of dhyāna, and
    that 'sitting in dhyāna' (in Japan: zazen) is the
    essence of Ch'an.
2. The expressions 'emptiness' and 'nirvāna' do not
    signify 'nothing' or 'absence'. 'Empty' means
    that all things are relative, that 'all dharmas
    are void of self-nature'. 'Nirvāna' which liter-
    ally means 'extinguished' (i.e. the end of all
    pain and frustration), is the negative way to
    point to the Absolute and is paraphrased as the
    'eternity, beatitude, selfhood and purity' of the
    Transcendent'. The term dharma means: entity,
    norm, thing, quality, concept, system or method,
    and Dharma: the Law, the Teaching or the Truth.
3. See Preface, pages 10-11.
4. Nan Hua-chin, whose quotations are not further
    identified, because of the great diversity of
    untranslated sources.
5. Nan Huai-chin.
6. His complete name is Ch'an master Ma-tsu Tao-i
    from Kiangsi (in Japanese: Baso Doitsu).
7. Yanagida Seizan, the leading figure in contempor-
    ary Ch'an studies in Japan, whose articles con-
    cerning Ma-tsu and the development of the recorded
    sayings are summarized in the following historical
    survey: Indogaku Bukkyogaku Kenkyu (or IBK) vol.
    17, no. 1 (1969), 33.
8. Ibid., 41-42.
9. Ui Hakuju, Zenshu shi kenkyu, vol. 1, p. 393.
10. See p. 83.

11. They mostly mention the long years of practice and study which preceded the sudden insight after which "one still followed the master for many years with daily progress in the mystery". . . (see for instance p. 82).

12. Lin-chi I-hsüan (Jap: Rinzi Gigen), died in 866, after whom the present Rinzai School in Japan is named. His recorded sayings have been translated by R.F. Sasaki, among others.

13. See p. 125.

14. Hui-neng (Jap: Eno), 638-713.

15. For example The Platform Scripture and the writings of Shen-hui.

16. Yanagida Seizan, op. cit.

17. For a review of his life (780-841) and work, see Jan Yün-hua, "Tsung-mi. His Analysis of Ch'an Buddhism" T'oung Pao, vol. 58 (1972), 1-54.

18. Huang-po Hsi-yün (Jap: Obaku Kiun), died in 850.

19. Kui-shan Ling-yu (Jap: Isan Reiyu) 771-853.

20. The Buddha's listeners were not only human beings on earth but also bodhisattvas and celestial beings, all together divided into eight classes.

21. Ch'an-yüan chu-ch'üan-chi tu-hsü. T. 2015, vol. 48, p. 399a.

22. This work is discussed by P. Demiéville in "Le Recueil de la Salle des Patriarches", T'oung Pao, vol. 56 (1970), 262-286.

23. T. 2076, vol. 51. Chang Chung-yüan translated nineteen biographies from this work in his Original Teachings of Ch'an Buddhism.

24. Nan-yüeh Huai-jang (Jap: Nangaku Ejo), 677-744.

25. Ho-tse Shen-hui (Jap: Kataku Jinne) 670-762. For a summary of his works, see Yampolski, Platform Sutra, pp. 24-25.

26. Shen-hsiu (Jap: Jinshu), 605-706.

27. The standard work in relation with the formation of the Platform Scripture and the Southern School is Yampolski's Platform Sutra. See also Wing-tsit Chan's translation: The Platform Scripture.

28. Hu Shih, "Ch'an Buddhism in China", Philosophy East and West, vol. 3 (1953), 12.

29. Ch'ing-yüan Hsing-ssu (Jap: Seigen Gyoshi), died in 740.

30. Shi-t'ou Hsi-ch'ien (Jap: Sekito Kisen), 700-791.

31. Sung kao-seng chuan, T. 2061, vol. 50, p. 764a.

32. See p. 112.

33. According to the Tsung-ching lu, T. 2016, vol. 48, p. 492a and 707b.

34. Nan-yang Hui-chung (died in 776), T. 2076, vol. 51, p. 438a.

35. Tsu-t'ang chi 15, 89, p. 288.

36. See for instance sections 5, 8, 14, 21.

37. Cited by Yanagida Seizan, IBK, vol. 18, no. 1 (1969) 40.

38. The appellation 'Recorded Sayings' (Yü-lu; Jap: goroku), has a rather late origin and appears for the first time in the Sung kao-seng chuan, T. 2061, vol. 50, p. 775 c 17. We refer to the preface for a definition of 'recorded sayings', kung-an (jap: koan) or 'public case' and 'dialogues' (wen-ta, jap: mondo).

39. yüan-wu k'e-ch'in (1063-1135) author of the Pi-yen lu or Blue Cliff Records (T. 2003, vol. 48).

40. Yanagida Seizan, loc. cit. pp. 41.42.

41. The extant text, included in the Continuation of the Canon, (HTC, 119; ZZ II.24.5, pp. 405-424, is a 1607 re-edition by Chieh Ning, also known as Ching-shan chü-shih from Tung-an. He probably

relied on the Kuang-teng-lu of 1063 (HTC 135. ZZ
II.B.8). The sections dealing with the four
masters, almost completely correspond with the
present Ming edition of the Ssu-chia yü-lu. There
are, however, various reasons to believe that the
Kuang-teng lu version, which served as a basis for
the present Ssu-chia yü-lu, goes back to an older
Ssu-chia yü-lu. The four masters are discussed in
much greater detail than the others, and Lin-chi's
role is totally different from his recorded sayings in the Tsung-ching lu and the Ch'üan-teng lu,
which are also integrally incorporated in the
Kuan-teng lu.

The most important versions of Ma-tsu's
Recorded Sayings appear in the Tsu-t'ang chi
(scroll 14), the Ch'üan-teng lu (scrolls 6 and
28), the Ssu-chia yü-lu (scroll 1), and the Ku-
tsun-su yü-lu (scroll 1). This last yü-lu collection: 'The Recorded Sayings of the Venerable
Elders' (HTC 118, ZZ II.23) translated by Lu
K'uan-Yü, The Transmission of the Mind, derives
from the Yang-ch'i school of the Lin-chi line.
The present text dates from 1267 and is based on
two editions of 1144 and 1238, which have been
lost. The Ssu-chia yü-lu contains all recorded
sayings which only partially appear in the other
sources. These four sources, however, present
almost identical texts. There is yet another
version, different from these four, which goes
back to a source older than the Tsu-t'ang chi,
namely the version in the Tsung-ching lu: the
Recordings of the Mirror of the School (T. 2016,
vol. 48).

This collection is not only a masterpiece of

Chinese literature, but also the most perfect compendium of and introduction to Chinese Buddhism. It is a product of the Fa-yen School, which emphasized doctrinal instruction. It contains a great number of recorded sayings of the Hung-chou School, and among those some statements of Ma-tsu's which appear nowhere else. We also discover in it the sayings which have later on been attributed to Nan-yüeh Huai-jang and Ch'ing-yüan Hsing-ssu.

We further refer to the Chih-yüeh lu; 'Records of Pointing toward the Moon' (HTC 143. ZZ II.B.16). This is one of the many collections of later date, but is in many respects valuable since it clarifies the theory as well as the practice of Ch'an, its insight as well as the cultivation. Moreover, it is not subject to the biases of one or other school. The most important kung-an collection is the Pi-yen lu (T. 2003, vol. 48) translated by Cleary, Sekida and others, and the Wu-men kuan (T. 2005, vol. 48) translated among others by Sekida.

42. In the SKSC, T. 2061, vol. 50, p. 766a-c, and in the Ch'üan T'ang wen, 501, XI, 6466-6467.

43. Ch'uan-teng lu, T. 2076, vol. 51, p. 236a.

44. T. 475, vol. 14, p. 539c, translated by Lu Kuan-yü, The Vimalakīrti Nirdesa Sutra, p. 20.

45. T. 235, vol. 8, p. 749a. 'Tathāgata' means literally 'Thus-gone' and is a common title for the Buddha.

46. T. 2076, vol. 51, p. 236; translated by P. Yampolski, p. 178.

47. P. Yampolski, p. 178.

48. The imagery of 'ground' (for mind) or 'seed' (for

doctrine) has also in Christianity many parallels; for example the parable of the sower; or Christ as 'Logos Spermaticus' by Justin the Martyr, de 'Soul-ground' in Ruusbroec, the 'ground' of existence in P. Tillich, etc.

49. T. 2076, vol. 51, p. 241a, and HTC 118, p. 80a-b.
50. T. 2076, vol. 51, p. 459, b1.
51. T. 2012, vol. 48, p. 382a. The latter expression is from the Lankāvatāra sūtra (T. 671, vol. 16, p. 574a).
52. Jimbo Nyoten, Zengaku jiten, p. 1099.
53. Nan Huai-chin.
54. D. T. Suzuki, Trans. The Lankāvatāra sūtra (T. 671, vol. 16); also see T. 670 and 672.
55. T. 1579, vo. 30.
56. T. 1509, vol. 25, partially translated by E. Lamotte, Le Traité de la Grande Vertu de Sagesse.
57. Translated by E. Conze, Buddhist Wisdom Books. A translation of the Chinese version (T. 235, vol. 8) with a commentary by Ch'an master Han-shan (HTC 39, pp. 112-140) can be found in Lu K'uan-yü, Chan and Zen Teachings, vol. 1.
58. This text has been translated by E. Lamotte, Lu K'uan-yü, R. Thurman, and others.
59. Lu K'uan-yü, Trans. p. 63.
60. R. Thurman, Trans. The Holy Teaching of Vimalakīrti, pp. 30-31.
61. T. 475, vol. 14, p. 542b.
62. The famous analogy used in the Lankāvatāra sūtra is that of water (reality) and waves (phenomena).
63. T.R.V. Murti, The Central Philosophy of Buddhism. London: George Allen & Unwin, 1960, (1st ed. 1955). 'Samsāra' means the cycle of birth and death.

64. Avatamsaka sūtra. T. 278, vol. 9; T. 279, and 293, vol. 10.

65. Thereupon he changed his approach: he started to teach his various listeners through different stages and on different levels, which was later the origin of the many schools within Buddhism. See for instance K. Ch'en, Buddhism in China (Princeton: Princeton University Press, 1964), pp. 305–311.

66. For a description of the Hua-yen school, see for instance Garma C.C. Chang. The Buddhist Teaching of Totality: The Philosophy of Hua Yen Buddhism. University Park: Pennsylvania State University Press, 1971; and F.H. Cook, Hua-yen Buddhism: the Jewel Net of Indra. University Park: Pennsylvania State University Press, 1977.

67. Jean Klein, lecture notes.

68. Nan Huai-chin.

69. J. Klein, Sois ce que tu es, pp. 51–52.

70. T. 945, vol. 19, Translated by Lu K'uan-yü.

71. T. 262, vol. 9, translated by L. Hurvitz, S. Murano and others.

72. T. 1666, vol. 32, translated by Y. S. Hakeda and others.

73. Nan Huai-chin.

74. T. 2061, vol. 50, p. 772.

75. These are expressions used in the Lotus sūtra and the Vimalakīrti-nirdeśa.

THE RECORDED SAYINGS OF
KIANGSI CH'AN MASTER TAO-I [1]

1. Biography

Section 1

Kiangsi Ch'an master Tao-i[2] was born in Shih-Fang[3]
county in Han-chou. His family name was Ma. He entered in the Lohan temple of that city. His appearance
was unusual. He walked like an ox and his gaze was as
a tiger's; his outstretched tongue reached beyond his
nose and on his soles he had two wheel-shaped figures.[4]
In his youth he was initiated by Reverend T'ang[5] from
Tzu-chou, and received full precepts[6] from Vinaya-
master Yüan from Yü-chou. During the K'ai-yüan period[7]
of the T'ang, he practiced concentration in the
Ch'üan-fa monastery on Moung Heng, where he met Reverend Jang.[8]

He knew that [Tao-i] was a 'dharma-vessel'[9] and
asked: 'Sir, what is your objective for sitting in
dhyāna?' The master said: 'I wish to become a Buddha'. Thereupon Jang took a brick and started to rub
it in front of his hut. The master said: 'Why do you
rub that brick?' Jang said: 'I'll polish it into a
mirror'. The master said: 'How can one polish a brick
into a mirror?' Jang said: 'If one cannot polish a
brick into a mirror, how can one become a Buddha by
sitting in dhyāna?' The master said: 'How should it
be done then?' Jang said: 'If one puts the ox to the
cart, and the cart does not move, who shall be beaten:
the cart or the ox?' The Master did not reply. Jang
further said: 'Is your purpose to learn how to sit in
dhyāna, or to learn how to sit in the Buddha? If you
learn how to sit in dhyāna, then dhyāna is neither

sitting nor lying. If you learn how to sit in the
Buddha, then the Buddha does not have any fixed characteristics. With regard to dharmas that do not stay, it
is better neither to grasp nor to reject. If you sit
in the Buddha, then you kill the Buddha. If you hold
on to the characteristics of sitting, you do not even
catch its principle'.

When the master heard this advice, it was as if he
had drunk ghee.[10] He bowed respectfully and asked:
'through what kind of mind effort can I reach the
samādhi without characteristics?'[11] Jang said: 'If
you seriously follow the method of the mind-ground, you
are like planting seeds; when I then explain the essentials of the dharmas, it is like rain falling from
heaven. Because your casual conditions all click, you
will certainly see the Path'.[12]

He further asked: 'If the Path does not have vis-
ible characteristics, how can it then be seen?' Jang
said: 'The dharma-eye[13] of the mind-ground is able to
see the Path. This also applies to the samādhi without
characteristics'. The master said: 'Is there achieving and failing?' Jang said: 'If one looks at the
Path in terms of achieving and failing, or of gathering
and dissipating, one does not see the Path. Listen to
my stanza:

The mind-ground contains numerous seeds,

When getting moisture, they all germinate.

The blossom of samādhi is characterless:

How could there be achieving or failing?

The master became awakened, beyond knowing and feeling.
He served [Jang] for ten years and progressed everyday
in the deep mysteries.

Earlier the Sixth Patriarch had said to Reverend
Jang that Prajñātāra from India has prophesied: 'under

your feet a colt will rise, which will trample down the people on earth'. He had meant the master.[14]

Jang had six disciples, of whom only the master secretly received the mind-seal. He first went from Mount Fo-chia-ling in Chien-yang to Lin-ch'üan, and next to Mount Kung-kung in Nan-k'ang[15]. During the Ta-li period, when he was registered at the K'ai-yüan temple in Chung-ling,[16] there was a general Lu Ssu-kung[17] who had heard about his reputation and fostered a deep admiration for him. He received personally his instruction in the doctrine. Thereupon from all four directions disciples gathered as clouds around his chair.

When Reverend Jang heard that the master was teaching in Kiangsi, he asked his followers 'Does Tao-i teach in public?' They answered: 'Yes'. Jang said: 'I have not met anyone yet to bring me news'. He then sent out a monk with this order: 'When he [Tao-i] enters into the hall[18] just ask him what he is doing. Wait for an answer and come to tell me.' As ordered, the monk went to ask him the question. The master answered: 'Ever since the disorder started with the barbarians thirty years ago, there has been no lack of pepper and salt'[19]. The monk returned and reported to Jang. Jang was satisfied.

The master had 139 disciples[20] who came to his room. Each of them became a local leader and spread the doctrine without end.

During the first month of the fourth year of the Chen-yüan period the master went up to the Shi-men mountain range in Chien-ch'ang. While he walked through the woods[21] he noticed a cave with an even floor. He said to his attendant: 'Next month my remains will return to this place.' Upon these words

he returned and soon manifested an illness.[22] When the
temple superintendent asked him: 'Reverend, how has
your health been lately?', the master answered: 'By
day in the face of the Buddha, at night in the face of
the Buddha'. The first day of the second month he took
a bath and sitting in the cross-legged position he
entered into nirvāna[23]. During the Yüan-huo period he
received the posthumous title of 'Ch'an master of Great
Silence' and an inscription on his stupa reads: 'Exalted Majesty'.[24]

2. Instructions

Section 2

Ma-tsu instructed his community as follows: 'Each of you, be convinced that your own mind is the Buddha. This mind is the Buddha. The great master Bodhidharma came from South India to China to transmit the doctrine of the one mind of the Supreme Vehicle, so that you may become awakened. He also used the Lankāvatāra sūtra as a guiding principle in order to seal the mind-ground in all beings, since he feared that you might capsize[25] and not believe in this dharma of the one mind, which is present in each of you. Therefore the Lankāvatāra sūtra says: 'in the proclamation of the Buddha, mind is the essence, and no-method is the teaching method. Whoever seeks the Dharma, should not seek anything. Outside the mind, there is no other Buddha; outside the Buddha, there is no other mind. Do not grasp good, do not reject evil; do not rely on the two extremes of pure and impure, understand that the nature of sin is empty. The succession of thoughts cannot be taken hold of[26] since they do not have a self-nature.   Therefore the triple world is only mind. All appearances in the universe are the impressions of the unique Dharma. Everything that is seen as form[27] is the seeing of the mind. The mind is not mind by itself but exists through forms. Whenever you speak, there is identity between phenomenon and principle without obstruction. This also applies to **bodhi**, the fruit of the Path[28]. What arises in the mind, is called form. Since you know that all forms are empty, arising is identical with non-arising.[29] If you understand the meaning of this, then you can at all times, whether you get dressed or chew your food, nourish the 'sacred embryo'[30] and

according to your destiny pass the time. What more is
there? You who receive my teaching, listen to my
stanza:

> The mind-ground speaks at all times,
> **Bodhi** always remains tranquil.
> Phenomena and principle do not obstruct each
> other,
> Arising is the same as non-arising.

Section 3

A monk asked: 'How should one cultivate the
Path?' He said: 'The Path does not need to be culti-
vated. If you say to attain through cultivation then
what is realized by it is again destroyed; then one is
like a śrāvaka. If you say not to cultivate, then one
is like an 'ordinary person'.

He further asked: 'Which mental attitude is
required for one to realize the Path?' Ma-tsu answered: 'The self-nature is originally perfect. Only
he who is not stuck between good and evil, may be
considered a practitioner of the Path. To grasp the
good and reject the evil, to contemplate emptiness and
enter into concentration, this belongs to intentional
action. If one, moreover, runs after externals, one
strays more and more. Completely exhaust the mind-
content of the triple world; since if one conceives of
only one erroneous thought, one generates the root of
birth-and-death and the triple world. If one only can
eliminate that one thought, one removes the root of
birth-and-death and one acquires the incomparable
treasure of the Dharma-king. Since endless kalpas[31]
the false imaginations, flattery and self-deception,
presumption and pride of the ordinary person all to-

gether form one substance. Therefore the scripture[32] says: 'This body is only a composition of a number of dharmas. When it arises, only the dharmas arise; when it ceases, only the dharmas cease. When these dharmas arise, they do not say "I arise"; when they cease, they do not say: "I cease". All thoughts, whether former, later or in between, have no mutual connection. The extinction of all thoughts is what is called 'the ocean-seal samādhi'[33]. All dharmas are contained in it, like hundreds of thousands of watercourses all discharging themselves into the wide ocean and are all called ocean water. They all have the same taste, which comprehends all tastes; they all are the wide ocean, which mixes all watercourses. If someone bathes in the ocean, he uses the water in its totality.

Therefore the awakening of a śrāvaka is delusion; while the ordinary person is deluded about awakening. The śrāvaka does not know that the mind of the saint[34] basically has no positions, nor degrees of causality. With false imaginations about the mind-content, he cultivates causes to realize effects while being stuck in empty concentration for 20,000 or 80,000 kalpas. Although he has been awakened, yet his awakening is a delusion. Bodhisattvas consider as (suffering) the tortures of hell to sink into emptiness and to be stuck in stillness, without seeing the Buddha nature. Someone with superior roots will run into a good and learned master[35] who will point him into the right direction. Under his explanation, he will gain insight, and no longer pass through positions and degrees, but be suddenly awakened to the original nature[36]. Therefore the scripture[37] says: 'The ordinary person has a flexible mind; the śrāvaka has not.'

This opposite of error is called awakening. But

since basically there is no error, there can be no
awakening either. All sentient beings have since
immeasurable kalpas never abandoned the samādhi of the
Dharma-nature[38]. They constantly are in the samādhi of
the Dharma-nature: their dressing and chewing, their
speaking and answering; the functioning of their six
faculties and all their deportments are ultimately
within this dharma-nature. Not knowing how to return
to the source, they pursue names and characters, so
that deluded feelings falsely arise and all kinds of
karma are created. If they could only for one moment
reflect[39] (their true nature), the whole essence would
become 'holy mind'. All of you penetrate to your own
true mind, and don't remember my words.

Even if you could proclaim as many principles of
the Path as there are grains of sand along the river
bank[40], it would not add anything to your mind; and if
you could not do so, it would not decrease your mind.
If you can explain, it is the mind; if you cannot, it
still is the mind. Even if you would multiply your
physical body, or radiate light, or manifest the eighteen bodily transformations, you still better return my
ashes. Sprinkled ashes do not have power, they are
like a śrāvaka who mistakenly cultivates causes to
produce results. Ashes which have not been sprinkled
do have power[41], like a bodhisattva whose karmic actions on the Path are pure and ripe, not stained by
evil. If you want to explain the Tathāgata's provi-
sional teachings in the Tripitaka, you will not finish,
even in a number of kalpas as many as there are grains
of sand in the riverbed. It is like a chain which is
never interrupted. But once you awaken to the mind of
the holy person, there is nothing else to do.

You have been standing a long time; go now and
take care.[42]

Section 4

He instructed the community as follows: 'There is
no need to cultivate the Path; only do not become
defiled.[43] What is to be defiled? A mind [discrimi-
nating] life and death, and the performing of deliberate actions is defilement. If you wish to understand
the Path, the ordinary mind is the Path. What is
called the ordinary mind? It is to be without deliberate actions, without distinguishing right and wrong,
grasping or rejecting, ordinary or holy. The scripture[44] says: 'Neither the action of the ordinary
person nor the action of the Saint is the bodhisattva-
action'. The Path ultimately is whether walking,
standing, sitting, or lying, to respond to the situation and to accept whatever happens. The Path is
identical with the Dharma-realm, to the point that none
of the wonderful functions, numerous as grains of sand,
falls outside the Dharma-realm. If it was not so, how
could one speak of the method of the mind-ground, or
speak of the inexhaustible lamp?[45] All dharmas are
mind-dharmas, all names are mind-names. The ten thousand dharmas all arise from the mind; or the mind is
the basic origin of the ten thousand things. The
scripture[46] says: 'If one's sincere mind penetrates to
the origin, one is called a 'śrāmana'. Whether names
or meanings, all dharmas are equal, pure and uncon-
fused. Whatever learning methods you happen to follow,
yet be independent at all times. If one establishes
[reality as][47] the Dharma-realm, then ultimately there
is the Dharma-realm; if one sees [reality] as True
Suchness, then ultimately there is True Suchness; if
one sees it as Principle, then it is Principle; if one

sees it as phenomena, then all dharmas are ultimately phenomena. If one presupposes one, a thousand will follow: principle and phenomena are without distinction; ultimately there only is wonderful functioning: there are no other principles. All derives from the turnings of the mind. It is like with the reflections of the moon: there appear a thousand of them, but in fact there is only one true moon. Or like water fountains: there are thousands of them; the nature of water, however, is only one. There are thousands of images great in majesty, but space is only one. There are thousands of ways to explain the Path, but unobstructed wisdom is only one. There are numerous types of positions, but all arise from the one mind. This applies to the establishing as well as to the discarding of positions. They are all wonderful functions, but ultimately all occur inside yourselves. It is not that outside the real there is room for positing anything: if anything is posited, it is the real, but it is the essence from inside yourselves. If it was not so, what kind of human beings would there be? All dharmas are Buddha-dharmas; all dharmas are emancipation; and emancipation is the same as True Suchness. No dharmas are outside True Suchness. Walking, standing, sitting and lying are all inconceivable functions which do not wait for a suitable time. The scripture[48] says: 'whatever place you can think of, there is the Buddha'. A Buddha is he who is capable of benevolence[49], who possesses wisdom, whose nature excels in capacity, who is able to tear up the net of doubts of sentient beings, and can free them from the bonds of being-and-not-being. For him feelings of ordinary and sacred have ceased to be; men and dharmas are all empty; he turns the unsurpassable wheel (of doctrine);

he transcends number and measure. In whatever he does
there is no obstacle; phenomena and principle are
mutually penetrating. As clouds arise in the sky:
suddenly they appear to disappear again without leaving
a trace. Or as writing on water: it does not arise
nor cease. This is the great Nirvāna: in bondage it
is called 'Tathāgata-womb'; out of bondage it is the
pure Dharma-kāya. This Dharma-kāya is infinite; its
essence cannot be increased or diminished. It can be
large or small, it may be round or square. Responding
to things, it appears in (many) shapes, like the moon
in water[50]: it flows in constant motion but does not
establish a firm basis. It does not exhaust action,
and does not dwell in non-action. Its action is the
personal function of non-action; non-action is the
personal support of action.[51] Since it does not dwell
on a support, it is said 'like the void it is without
any suppport'.[52] The significance of 'the mind causes
arising and ceasing', is the meaning of the mind's True
Suchness. The mind's True Suchness can be compared to
a clear mirror which reflects images. The mirror
symbolizes the mind; the images symbolize the dharmas.
If the mind grasps the dharmas, there is involvement
with external causality: that is the meaning of arising and ceasing. If the mind does not grasp dharmas,
that means True Suchness. The śrāvaka hears about the
Buddha-nature; but the bodhisattva perceives it. He
fathoms the non-duality, which is called the universal
nature. This nature is without diversity, but in its
functioning there is no uniformity. In error it oper-
ates as consciousness; in awakening it acts as wisdom.
To follow reality is awakening; to follow phenomena is
to be deluded. Delusion is to err about one's own
original mind; to be awakened is to realize one's own

original nature.   Once awakened, one remains awakened
without return to delusion. As the raising of the sun
dispels darkness,   so   can the   rising   of the   sun   of
wisdom not go together with the darkness of contaminations.[53] If one   understands the mind and its   object-
realm, erroneous thoughts will not arise. If erroneous
thoughts do not arise, there is the acceptance of
non-arising.[54]

What is basically present, is present now and does
not depend on cultivating the Path or sitting in
dhyāna. Not to cultivate and not to sit, that is the
pure dhyāna of the Tathāgata.[55] If today you perceive
the truth and correctness of this principle, you do not
create any more karma and lead a life allotted to you,
even, with only one robe and one jacket. Sitting and
rising follow each other, while you mature in the
observation of the rules and increase your pure karma.
If only you are able to do this, why be concerned about
not fully understanding?

You have been standing here a long time, folks; go
now and take care.

3. Dialogues

Section 5

One time Hsi-t'ang, Pai-chang and Nan-ch'üan[56] accompanying Ma-tsu, looked at the moon. Ma-tsu said: 'How is it right now?'

Hsi-t'ang said: 'Just right for reverence.'

Pai-chang said: 'Just right for cultivation.'

Nan-ch'üan shook down his sleeve[57] and left.

Ma-tsu said: 'The scriptures are in Tsang. Dhyāna belongs to Hai. Only P'u-yüan transcends all things.' (Hsi-t'ang Tsang, Pai-chang Hai, Nan-ch'üan Yüan).[58]

Section 6

Once Nan-ch'üan served rice-gruel to the community of monks. Ma-tsu asked: 'What is in the pot?'[59] Ch'üan said: 'Wish that that old man would keep his mouth, what does he mumble there?' Ma-tsu did not react.

Section 7

Pai-chang asked: 'What is the essence of Buddhism?'

Ma-tsu said: 'It is precisely where you let go of your life.'

Section 8

When Ta-chu[60] first joined Ma-tsu, Ma-tsu asked: 'Where do you come from?' He said: 'From the Ta-yün monastery in Yüeh-chou.'

Ma-tsu asked: 'What is your intent to come here?' Ta-chu said: 'I come to look for the Buddha's teaching.'

Ma-tsu said: 'You do not care for the treasury in yourself. What is the use of abandoning your family and become a vagrant? Here I do not have anything at all. What kind of Buddha teaching are you looking for?'

Thereupon Chu bowed respectfully and asked: 'What is that, Hui-hai's own treasury?'

Ma-tsu said: 'Precisely that what just asked me, that is your treasury: everything is there, nothing is missing. Use it freely; why should you still go and look outside?'

With these words Chu became aware of his original mind, beyond knowing and feeling. He danced with joy and bowed gratefully. He stayed six years with the master, and then returned. He wrote a "Treatise on the Essentials of Entering the Path through Sudden Awakening", in one volume.

After Ma-tsu had seen it, he declared to his group: 'In Yüeh-chou there is a "great pearl", perfectly clear, transparent and free, without any imperfection.'

Section 9

Ch'an master Le-t'an Fa-hui asked Ma-tsu: 'What is the significance of the Master Patriarch's coming from the West?'[61]

Ma-tsu said: 'Be quiet! Come closer by.' Hui came closer and Ma-tsu boxed him on the ear, and said: 'Among six ears one does not scheme plots.[62] Come back tomorrow.'

Hui returned the next day, entered the dharma hall[63] and said: 'Please, Reverend, explain.'

Ma-tsu said: 'Go away for a while. Wait until the old one ascends the hall and step forward. Then I'll testify for you.'

Thereupon Hui was awakened and said: 'I thank this great community for its testimony.' He made once the round of the hall and left.

Section 10

One day Ch'an master Le-t'an Wei-chien sat in dhyāna behind the dharma hall. Ma-tsu noticed him and went to blow twice in his ear. Chien rose from his concentration, noticed it was Ma-tsu and went back into concentration. Ma-tsu went to his room and sent a servant with a cup of tea to Chien. Chien ignored it but returned to the hall.

Section 11

Ch'an master Shih-kung Hui-tsang[64] was originally a professional hunter and had an aversion for monks. Once pursuing a herd of deer he passed by Ma-tsu's cottage. Ma-tsu went to meet him and Tsang asked: 'Reverend, did you see any deer pass by here?'

Ma-tsu asked: 'Who are you?'

He said: 'A hunter.'

Ma-tsu asked: 'Do you know how to shoot?'

He said: 'Yes, I know.'

Ma-tsu asked: 'How many can you shoot with one arrow?'

He said: 'With one arrow I shoot one.'

Ma-tsu said: 'You do not know how to shoot.'

He asked: 'Does   your   reverence   know   how   to
shoot?'

Ma-tsu said: 'Yes, I do.'

He asked: 'How   many does   your reverence   shoot
with one arrow?'

Ma-tsu said: 'With one   arrow,   I can   shoot   a
herd.'

He said: 'They   are living beings as well as   we:
why would you shoot a whole herd of them?'

Ma-tsu asked: 'If   you know this, why do you   not
shoot at yourself?'

He said: 'Though you tell me to shoot at   myself,
I would not even know how to go about it.'

Ma-tsu said: 'This fellow!   Ignorance and defilement for kalpas suddenly cease today!'

At that moment Tsang broke his bow and arrows   and
cut off his   hair   with   his sword.[65]   He submitted   to
Ma-tsu and became a monk.

One day when he was at work in the kitchen, Ma-tsu
asked him: 'What are you doing?'

He said: 'Herding the ox.'[66]

Ma-tsu asked: 'Herding?'

He said: 'As soon as he runs back to the grass, I
pull him out by his nostrils.'

Ma-tsu said: 'You really herd the ox.'

Section 12

A monk asked Ma-tsu: 'Reverend, may I ask you   to
point directly out to me the meaning of the coming from
the West, ignoring the four assertions and the   hundred
negations?'[67]

Ma-tsu said: 'I do not feel   like it today.   Go
and ask Chih-tsang.'

The monk then asked Tsang.

Tsang said: 'Why do you not go and ask the master?'

The monk said: 'He told me to come and ask you.'

Tsang rubbed his hand over his head and said: 'I've got a head-ache today.   Go and ask my colleague Hai.'

The monk again went to ask Hai.

Hai said: 'I do not understand this.'

Thereupon the monk went to report everything to Ma-tsu.

Ma-tsu said: 'Tsang's head is white, Hai's head is black.'[68]

Section 13

One day Ch'an master Ma-ku Pao-ch'e accompanied Ma-tsu on a walk and asked: 'What is the great nir-vana?'

Ma-tsu said: 'Hurry!'

Ch'e asked: 'Hurry for what?'

Ma-tsu said: 'Look at the water.'[69]

Section 14

When Ch'an master Fa-ch'ang from Mount Ta-mei[70] at first joined Ma-tsu, he asked: 'What is the Buddha?'

Ma-tsu said: 'The mind is the Buddha.'   Thereupon Ch'ang was greatly awakened. Later he went to live on Mount Ta-mei.[71]

When Ma-tsu heard that the master resided on the mountain, he sent out a monk to ask: 'Reverend, when you met Master Ma, what did you gain that made you come and stay on this mountain?'

Ch'ang said: 'Master Ma has told me: The mind is the Buddha, and then I came to live here.'

The monk said: Lately Ma-tsu's Buddha teaching has changed again.'

Ch'ang said: 'What has changed?'

The monk answered: 'Lately he has been saying: neither the mind, nor the Buddha.'

Ch'ang said: 'That old fellow misleads people without end! I have nothing against your 'neither the mind, nor the Buddha', but I stick to 'the mind is the Buddha'.'

The monk returned the report to Ma-tsu.

Ma-tsu said: 'The plum is ripe.'

Section 15

Ch'an master Wu-yeh[72] from Fen-chou joined Ma-tsu. Ma-tsu observed his elegant appearance and bell-like voice, and said: 'What an impressive Buddha-hall! Too bad there is no Buddha in it.'

Yeh knelt in reverence and said: 'The literature of the Three Vehicles[73] I can roughly make out. But I often hear talk about the Ch'an teaching 'the mind is the Buddha' and I just fail to understand.'

Ma-tsu said: 'Precisely the mind that fails to understand, that is it; there further is nothing.'

Yeh went on asking: 'What is the mind-seal which the Master Patriarch from the West has secretly transmitted?'

Ma-tsu said: 'Reverend, you busy yourself too much. You better go now and come back another time.'

Yeh was on his way out, when Ma-tsu called: 'Reverend!' (Great Virtue!)

Yeh turned his head. Ma-tsu said: 'What is it?'

Yeh right then became awakened and bowed in reverence.

Ma-tsu said: 'You rascal! Why do you bow?'

Section 16

Teng Yin-Feng[74] came to bid farewell from Ma-tsu.
Ma-tsu said: 'Where are you going?'
He said: 'I'm going to Shih-t'ou.' [lit. 'Stone']
Ma-tsu said: 'A stone-path is slippery.'
He said: 'I am carrying a staff with me and can play along all right,'[75] and left.

As soon as he arrived at Shih-t'ou, he made one round of the meditation-seats, shook his staff once and asked: 'What is here the basic stuff?'
T'ou said: 'Good Heavens! Good Heavens!'
Feng was speechless and returned to Ma-tsu to report.

Ma-tsu said: 'Go back, and see if he will say 'Good Heavens! Good Heavens!' again. Then whistle twice.'

Feng went back. As soon as he had asked his question as before, T'ou whistled twice. Teng was speechless again and returned to report to Ma-tsu.

Ma-tsu said: 'I had warned you that the stone-path was slippery!'

Section 17

One day Feng was pushing a wheelbarrow. Ma-tsu was sitting across the path with stretched legs. Feng said: 'Would the master please draw in his feet?'
Ma-tsu said: 'What is already stretched cannot be drawn in.'

Feng said: 'What is already going forward cannot go backward' and pushed the wheelbarrow over the master's legs.

With hurting legs, Ma-tsu returned to the dharma-hall. He held an axe and said: 'Let the one who has just hurt this old monk's legs come forward!'

Feng stepped forward and stretched his neck out in front of Ma-tsu.

Ma-tsu then put the axe away.

Section 18

When monk Shih-chiu[76] first joined Ma-tsu, Ma-tsu asked: 'Where do you come from?'

Chiu said: 'I come from Wu-chiu.'

Ma-tsu said: 'What has Wu-chiu lately been saying?'

Chiu said: 'Some people there are rather befuddled.'

Ma-tsu said: 'Let's not talk about being befuddled. How do you feel about a 'silent statement'?'

Thereupon Chiu made three steps forward.

Ma-tsu said: 'I'd like to send to Wu-chiu seven canings. Are you prepared?'

Chiu said: 'Reverend, if you receive them first, I am prepared to be next.' He then returned to Wu-chiu.

Section 19

Instructor Liang came to visit Ma-tsu.

Ma-tsu asked: 'I've it from hearsay that the Instructor is very eloquent in explaining the sutras and commentaries. Is that true?'

Liang said: 'You flatter me!'

Ma-tsu said: 'How do you lecture?'

Liang said: 'With the mind.'

Ma-tsu said: 'The mind is like an artist; knowledge like its assistant[77]; how can you interpret the scriptures with the mind?'

Liang protested and said: 'If the mind cannot explain, is empty space doing it?'

Ma-tsu said: 'Right, it is precisely emptiness that explains.'

Liang disagreed and left.

Just about going down the steps, Ma-tsu called: 'Instructor!' Liang turned around and was suddenly greatly awakened. He bowed respectfully. Ma-tsu said: 'You stupid teacher, why do you bow?'

Liang returned to his temple and told his audience: 'I presumed that nobody was my equal in interpreting the scriptures. Today as the great teacher Ma asked one question, my whole life's work melted as ice and crumbled as pottery!'

He went straight to the western mountains and disappeared without a trace.

Section 20

When monk Shui-lao from Hung-chou first joined Ma-tsu, he asked: 'What is the purpose of the coming from the West?'

Ma-tsu said: 'Bow down.' As Lao was bowing, Ma-tsu gave him a kick. Lao had a great awakening. He stood up, clapped his hands, and laughed loud 'Ha! Ha!' saying: 'How wonderful! How wonderful! A hundred thousand samādhis and an infinite number of mysterious truths all have their origin on the tip of a hair!'[78]

He then bowed respectfully and withdrew.

Later he said to the community: 'From the time when I received Master Ma's kick until now, I cannot stop laughing.'

Section 21

Layman P'ang[79] asked Ma-tsu: 'What kind of a person is he who is not a companion of the ten thousand dharmas?'

Ma-tsu said: 'Wait till you have drained in one gulp all the water of the Western river, then I shall tell you.' He further asked Ma-tsu: 'Please, Master, look highly up at someone who is not blind for the origin.' Ma-tsu looked downward. The layman said: 'A kind of lute without strings which only the master can play perfectly.' The master looked upward. The layman bowed. Ma-tsu returned to his rooms. The layman followed him inside: 'I just now tried to be clever, but turned out to be clumsy.'

He asked: 'What do you think of water: it has no muscles and no bones, and can yet carry a ship of a hundred thousand bushels?'

Ma-tsu said: 'There is no water around here, and no boat either; what muscles and bones are you talking about?'

Section 22

A monk asked: 'Reverend, why do you say: the mind is the Buddha?'

Ma-tsu said: 'To make children stop crying.'[80]

He said: 'When the crying stops, what then?'

Ma-tsu said: 'It is neither the mind nor the Buddha.'

He said: 'If someone different from these two comes, how do you teach them?'

Ma-tsu said: 'To him I say: it is not a thing.'

He said: 'And if suddenly some insider comes, what then?'

Ma-tsu said: 'Him I teach to realize the essence of the great Path.'

Section 23

Somebody asked: 'What is the meaning of the coming from the West?'

Ma-tsu: 'What does that mean right now?'

Section 24

A monk asked: 'How can one obtain oneness with Tao?'

Ma-tsu said: 'I am since long not one with Tao.'

Someone asked: 'What is the meaning of the coming from the West?'

Ma-tsu gave him a blow and said: 'If I do not give you a blow, everybody will laugh at me.'

Section 25

There once was a young teacher, Tan-yüan[81], who returned from a traveling tour[82]. In front of Ma-tsu he drew a circle[83], he bowed and stood in it.

Ma-tsu said: 'You wish to become a Buddha, don't you?'

He said: 'I do not know how to rub my eyes.'[84]

Ma-tsu said: 'I am not a match for you.'

The young teacher gave no answer.

Section 26

There once was a monk who in front of Ma-tsu drew four lines. The upper line was longer, the three lines underneath shorter.

He said: 'Without arguing that one line is longer and three lines are shorter, leaving aside the four assertions and the hundred negations, may I ask your Reverence to answer me.'

Thereupon Ma-tsu drew one line on the ground and said: 'Without arguing about long and short, there is your answer.'

Section 27

Ma-tsu sent a monk with a special delivery letter to Reverend Ch'in of Ching-shan[85]. In the letter he had drawn a circle. As soon as Ching-shan opened the letter and saw, he asked for a brush and dotted a point in the middle. Later on a monk told this to National Master Chung.[86] Master Chung said: 'Master Ch'in has been deceived again by Master Ma.'

Section 28

Once a preacher came with this question: 'May I ask what kind of doctrine the Ch'an school holds and spreads?'

Ma-tsu asked in turn: 'And you, instructor, which doctrine do you hold and spread?'

The instructor said: 'Your servant can explain over twenty sutras and commentaries.'

Ma-tsu said: 'You are a lion, aren't you?[87]'

The instructor said: 'You flatter me.'

Ma-tsu whistled a few times.

The instructor said: 'That is the doctrine.'

Ma-tsu said: 'What doctrine?'

The instructor said: 'The doctrine of the lion coming out of his den.'

Ma-tsu remained silent.

The instructor said: 'This also is the doctrine.'

Ma-tsu said: 'What doctrine?'

The instructor said: 'The doctrine of the lion staying in his den.'

Ma-tsu said: 'Not to come out and not to go in[88], what doctrine is that?'

The instructor was speechless; he said farewell and left.

Ma-tsu called: 'Instructor!'

The instructor turned his head.

Ma-tsu said: 'What is it?'

The instructor remained speechless.

Ma-tsu said: 'What a stupid instructor!'

Section 29

The imperial prosecutor of Hung-chou asked: 'Is one allowed to take wine and meat?'

Ma-tsu said: 'If you take them, it is your excellency's rank (lu); if you do not, it is your excellency's good luck (fu).'

Section 30

When Ch'an master Yao-shan Wei-yen[89] first joined Shih-t'ou, he asked: 'The Three Vehicles and the Twelve Divisions of the Teaching[90], I roughly understand; but I often hear that in the South one directly points at man's mind in order to see one's nature and to become a Buddha. I really do not get it. I pray to you, Reverend, to be compassionate and explain it to me.'

T'ou said: 'Like-this does not work; not-like-this does not work either; like-this or not-like-this, do not work in any case. What do you make of it?' Shan was perplexed.

T'ou said: 'Your affinity is not here; you better go to great Master Ma.'

Shan followed the advice. He went to pay his respect to Ma-tsu and asked his question as before.

Ma-tsu said: 'Sometimes I teach him to raise his eyebrows and to twinkle his eyes, sometimes I do not teach him to raise his eyebrows and to twinkle his eyes. Sometimes to raise the eyebrows and to twinkle the eyes is right, sometimes to raise the eyebrows and to twinkle the eyes is not right. What do you make of that?'

With these words Shan became awakened and made a bow.

Ma-tsu said: 'What kind of truth did you perceive to make you bow?'

Shan said: 'At Shih-t'ou's place I felt like a mosquito on an iron ox.'

Ma-tsu said: 'If you feel like that, look after yourself carefully.'

For three years Shan stayed in his service.

One day Ma-tsu asked him: 'How has it lately been with your insight?'

Shan said: 'I have completely thrown off my skin. There is only one true reality.'

Ma-tsu said: 'What you have obtained can be said

to be in harmony with the essence of the mind, and reaches out to your four limbs. Since that is the case, go and get three bamboo plaits, tie them around your middle and go to live somewhere in the mountains.'

Shan said: 'Who am I that I'd presume to live on a mountain!'

Ma-tsu said: 'Not so. Walking cannot go on forever without stopping, stopping cannot go on forever without walking. If you wish to improve where there is nothing to improve, if you wish to act where there is nothing to act, it would be suitable to become a vessel[91] and not to stay here any longer.'

Shan then said farewell to Ma-tsu.

Section 31

Ch'an master Tan-hsia T'ien-jan[92] again joined Ma-tsu. Before he went in to pay his respects, he went to the monks' hall, where he climbed onto the head of Mañjuśrī[93] and sat down. The whole community was struck with amazement, and Ma-tsu was informed immediately. Ma-tsu went to the hall to see for himself and said:

'My disciple is spontaneous.' (T'ien-jan)

Hsia came down, bowed respectfully and said: 'Thank you, Master, for giving me a religious name.'[94]

Therefore he is called T'ien-jan (spontaneous).

Section 32

When Ch'an master T'an-chou Hui-lang first joined Ma-tsu, Ma-tsu asked: 'What do you come looking for?'

He said: 'I am looking for the knowledge and the seeing of the Buddha.'[95]

Ma-tsu said: 'The Buddha is without knowing and seeing. Knowing and seeing are evil spirits. Where do you come from?'

He said: 'From Nan-yüeh.'[96]

Ma-tsu said: 'You come from Nan-yüeh and do not know the essence of the mind of Ts'ao-hsi? Return there fast, it is of no use to go anywhere else.'

Section 33

Ma-tsu once asked a monk: 'Where do you come from?'

He said: 'From Hunan.'

Ma-tsu said: 'Is the water of the East lake full yet?'[97]

He said: 'Not yet.'

Ma-tsu said: 'It has been raining a long time, why is it not full yet?'

(Tao-wu says: 'It is full.'

Yun-yen says: It is very deep.'

Tung-shan says: 'During which kalpa has there ever been a shortage?')[98]

NOTES

1. For a general discussion of the text, see <u>Intro-duction</u>, pp. 45-68. The subtitles and the division into sections in this translation are not found in the Chinese original.

2. The Ch'an masters are usually named after the location (temple or monastery, mountain or region) where they have been especially operating. This is sometimes followed by their religious name. For example, Lin-chi I-hsüan is generally known as Master Lin-chi. 'I-hsüan' is his religious name; Lin-chi is the name of the temple and the place where he established himself as master. Similarly, Ma-tsu's official name is Kiangsi Tao-i. 'Kiangsi' is the name of the province in southeast China where Ma-tsu was active and where Ch'an Buddhism reached a high level of development during the T'ang dynasty. 'Tao-i' (or 'Tao-One') is the religious name which he received at the time of ordination. Kiangsi Tao-i is generally called 'Ma-tsu', which literally means 'Patriarch or Ancestor Ma'. 'Ma' (horse) is a widely spread family name. It does, however, never or rarely happen that a Buddhist monk is called with his secular name. Probably Hui-neng's prophecy about a 'young horse' (**ma-chü**) has contributed to this (see p. 83). '**Tsu**' or 'ancestor' is derived from the Chinese ancestor cult and has been adopted into Buddhism to denominate the founders, leaders or patriarchs of various schools comparable to 'religious founder' or 'Church Father' in Christianity.

3. This county (**hsien**) was located to the south of the present Shih-fang **hsien** and is now called

Kuang-han **hsien** to the north of Ch'eng-tu in the province of Szuchuan. There is no certainty about Ma-tsu's date of birth. Generally the year 709 has been accepted. Ui Hakuju, however, prefers 707. (see note 23, p. 116)

4.   This is a typical description of a very important personage in classical Chinese biographies. The impression is made that we have to do with someone who inaugurated a new era. The large tongue and the wheelshaped figures on his footsoles, are, moreover, two physical marks of excellence proper to a Buddha or a great person. Relating to his extraordinary appearance, the memoirs of Chüan Te-yü (see p. 77 note 42) say that "he did not participate in childrens' games during his youth. He was impressive as a mountain, clear and deep as a quiet river. His perfect virtue and disposition to the Dharma had been given to him by Heaven..." The Sung Kao-seng chuan (abbr.: SKSC) gives a similar hagiographic account.

5.   This is nobody less than Ch'u-chi (648-734), successor of Chih-hsien (609-702). (See p. 45).

6.   Namely the 250 rules of monastic life, to be observed after final ordination, which should, according to the Vinaya, be administered at the age of twenty.

7.   The years 713 till 741 during the reign of emperor Hsüan-tsung.

8.   Heng-yüeh or Heng-shan, located in the north of Heng-yang county, in Hunan province, is one of the five sacred mountains of China; it is also called Nan-yüeh (Southern Peak). Hence is derived Jang's full name: Nan-yüeh Huai-jang (677-744). According to later history, Jang had already been living

for fifteen years on Heng-yüeh, in the Prajñā temple, when Ma-tsu arrived there in 734, after the death of his master Ch'u-chi. According to the Ku-tsun-su yü-lu, Ma-tsu had isolated himself in a hut near the Ch'üan-fa temple, where he practiced meditation without ever paying attention to anybody. When Jang once came to visit him, he was likewise ignored; but struck by his unusual appearance he recalled Hui-neng's prophecy. He tried in various ways to seduce Ma-tsu to engage in conversation, and so started to rub a brick, whereupon Ma-tsu only after a long time reacted.

About this encounter between Nan-yüeh and Ma-tsu nothing is mentioned either in Nan-yüeh's or in Ma-tsu's historic chronicles. The Tsu-t'ang chi only narrates the brick incident and the stanza uttered by Nan-yüeh. The Ch'uan-teng lu adds to this that Ma-tsu became awakened and remained for ten years in the service of Nan-yüeh. Both versions have presumably been inspired by the Pao-lin chuan and were preceded by the Tsung-ching lu. It appears therefore that the Ma-tsu 'history' had been complemented at an early date, due to the image of Ma-tsu which took shape in the Hung-chou School.

9. Dharma-vessel is an expression which also occurs in the encounter between Bodhidharma, the Founder and first patriarch of Ch'an, and his successor: After Hui-k'o had cut off his arm, the master knew that he was a dharma-vessel. The term indicates the aptitude to 'contain' the Dharma.

10. A kind of nectar distilled from butter, used in India for ceremonial purposes. In Buddhism it is an image of perfect truth.

11. "What is the **samādhi** **without** **characteristics** (**ānimitta-samādhi**)? All dharmas are without marks. Not to accept and not to reject any dharmas, that is the **samādhi** without characteristics. As it is said in a stanza: When words have come to rest, the activities of the mind also disappear. Neither arising nor ceasing, it is an image of **nirvāna**." (T. 1509, vol. 25, p. 96c)

12. The seeing of 'emptiness' as true nature, is in Ch'an terminology 'to understand the mind and to see nature'. 'When one sees seeing, then seeing is not this seeing. Seeing is even separate from seeing and cannot be reached through seeing.' (Śūrangama sūtra). The seeing of Tao, in other words, is the seeing of what sees and has nothing to do with everything that could be seen.

13. The dharma-eye signifies a bodhisattva's power to penetrate the dharma of causal existence and to review all means to save sentient beings. The dharma-eye is latent in everyone and is opened at the moment of conversion. A stereotyped description of it is as follows: "In him the dharma-eye awoke, dustless and spotless, and he recognized that everything which has arising as its law (dharma), also has ceasing as its law." (E. Lamotte, L'Enseignement de Vimalakīrti, p. 124).

14. Hui-neng's prophecy made to Nan-yüeh (Jang) with reference to Ma-tsu, can be interpreted in this way: 'Among your followers Ma-tsu (**ma-chü** or colt) will arise, and his school will overshadow all other schools.'

    Prajñātāra, the 27th Indian Patriarch, is believed to have prophesied to his successor Bodhidharma, the first Chinese Patriarch, the coming of both Nan-yüeh Huai-jang and Ma-tsu.

The Tsu-t'ang chi in its text (and commentary) has a different version of the same prophecy: "Although Chen-tan has a vast expanse, yet there is not another way ('Chen-tan' is China; 'not another way': there is only the teaching of the one mind, as it has been proclaimed by great Master Jang), through which one shall follow posterity's footsteps ('posterity': the present successors of the teaching). A golden rooster will in his beak bring along a grain of rice ('golden rooster': Master Jang was born in Chin-chou, the 'golden prefecture'; with 'one grain of rice' is meant Tao-i since Ma-tsu from Kiangsi is called Tao-i or 'One'), to offer to the Lohan monk from Shih-fang. (Reverend Jang transmitted the teaching to Tao-i; that is why 'to offer' is mentioned; Shih-fang: Master Ma became a monk in the Lohan temple of Shih-fang county in Han-chou.)

This prophecy originally consisted of eight verses instead of four and was included in the lost scroll of #7 of the Pao-lin chuan. In the Ku-tsun-su yü-lu, there are eight verses:
"Although Chen-tan has a vast expanse . . .
The Dharma which can comprehend the mind
Will be proclaimed on the river bank in Han;
the waves on the lake look at the moon in the water, which will awaken two or three persons."

(HTC 118, p. 79d)

These verses too have been traditionally inter-preted as referring to Ma-tsu, since he originated from the Han prefecture. However, the prophecy about the colt is in this text attributed to

Hui-neng himself, as is the case in the Ch'üan teng lu, where Hui-neng adds:

"Conserve all this in your mind;
Do not speak of it too lightly."

(T. 2076, vol. 51, p. 240c)

15. The county **Chien-yang** belongs today to Chien-an-tao in Fukien province. In some biographies of his disciples, this mountain is being mentioned as one of Ma-tsu's residences but it is not known how long he stayed there. In 743-744 he already was in **Lin-ch'üan**, in the prefecture of Fu-chou of Kiangsi province. **Nan-k'ang** probably is a county in Kan-nan-tao in southern Kiangsi. The mountain Kung-kung is situated in the northeast of present Kan-chou. According to Hsi-t'ang's biography (Section 5, p. 93) in the Ch'üan-teng lu and the SKSC, Hsi-t'ang followed Ma-tsu to this mountain. There the master attracted some other disciples, such as Pai-chang (Section 5, p. 87). When Ma-tsu approached this mountain, thus the SKSC narrates, "the grottoes were densely populated with evil spirits. No human being had the nerve to approach them, and whoever took the risk anyway, was immediately harassed. As soon as he had settled there, a spirit in purple garment and wearing a dark hat came to greet him: 'I give up this territory so that it might be a pure place'. After these words it disappeared, and from then onward the cruel and poisonous animals of the area became tame and obedient." (T. 2061, vol. 50, p. 766a-b).

16. According to Ui Hakuju, Ma-tsu already established himself for good in Hung-chou, Northern Kiangsi, during the first or second year of the Ta-li

period (766-779). Hung-chou was situated in present-day Nan-ch'ang county, in the northwest of **Chung-ling**. These three locations (Hung-chou, Nan-ch'ang and Chung-ling) are used alternatively to indicate the place of Ma-tsu's activities, and where his school, called the Hung-chou School, took its origin.

17. His original name was Lu Chien-k'o. Emperor Hsüan-tsung (713-756) gave him the name Ssu-kung and appointed him as the inspector of Kiangsi.

18. Literally 'to ascend the hall'. This is an expression used for the formal instruction which took place upon a podium in the dharma-hall (See section 9, pp. 104-105 and note 64, p. 127). These instructions were usually held in the form of a lively conversation with the audience; therefore a dialogue like this one was not uncommon.

19. Here is probably referred to the An Lu-shan rebellion (755-763) which had cut off the supply routes of spices and similar items.

20. The Ch'üan-teng lu also mentions 139 successors and contains biographies for 75 of them. Besides, of 63 others only the names are given. The SKSC further mentions several successors, which do not appear in the CTL. Yanagida Seizan feels that the CTL has a tendency to exaggerate the number; he holds that certainly eighty disciples 'entered into his room'. This is also the number of 'good masters' (kalyānamitra) attested by Huang-po and Kui-shan.

21. 'To practice the walking meditation' is a Buddhist expression (cañkrama) indicating the well-defined exercise of walking, intended to prevent indisposition or drowsiness during prolonged meditation,

or to recover from sickness. Thus for example one reads in the Lotus sūtra: "I notice bodhisattvas who do not sleep, walk in the forest (practice the walking meditation)." (T. 262, vol. 9, p. 3b).

22. This expression is used when a Buddha, a bodhisattva or an eminent monk **manifests an illness** in their physical body. An Enlightened One is 'pure' and therefore cannot become 'ill'. Phenomena of illness are nothing but contingent phenomena, which do not affect at all an Enlightened Being. About Vimalakīrti is said that he possessed a limitless capacity in using methods of salvation. Through one of these methods, he 'manifested an illness'."

23. According to Ch'üan Te-yü, who was a student of Ma-tsu during the final years of his life, the Master died in the 4th month of the 2nd year **Chen-yüan** (785-804), at the age of 80; from which one may conclude that Ma-tsu lived from 707 till 787. The SKSC and all other sources, however, state the 4th year, and also the age of 80 ('religious' age of 60), so that the general consensus about his dates is 709-789. According to the SKCS his funeral was incredibly splendid; 'light and darkness took turns' people came from far away places, so that the oars covered the water as if turning it into land; lanterns burnt until daybreak; presents accumulated in great numbers; the smell of food offered to the monks by the population penetrated everywhere. . .' His funeral is further compared with another one that ruined the land, i.e. Pu-chi's (died in 739), Shen-hsiu's successor in the northern Ch'an school (T. 2061, vol. 50, p. 766b).

24. During the **Yüan-huo** period (806-820) he received this title from emperor Hsien-tsung. Originally the custom of receiving honorary titles after death was reserved to emperors and great ministers. For Buddhism it was the equivalent of 'canonization' of great masters. Ma-tsu's stupa with the stone inscription by Ch'üan Te-yü was located on mount Shih-men.

25. Literally 'upside down'. This expression points to the fundamental error "which is the origin of the suffering and erring predicament in which sentient beings find themselves since times immemorial". "Due to ignorance (**avidyā**) the ordinary person attributes to all dharmas an opposite (erroneous) character. What is impermanent, he sees as permanent; what is painful he sees as joyful; what has no self, he invests with a self; what is empty, he holds as real; what does not exist, he sees as existing; and what exists as non-existing". (From the MPPS, T. 1509, vol. 24, p. 171c). Conze translates this term as 'upset: often translated as "perverted views". This does not affect the meaning, because we can never be upset by any fact, but only by our wrong interpretations of it. . . Akin to ignorance, the root evil, they can be viewed as mis-searches (looking for permanence, etc. in the wrong place), or mistakes, or reversals (of the truth), or as overthrowers of inner calm'. (Buddhist Wisdom Books, p. 97).

26. Literally 'thought after thought is un-graspable', or 'moment after moment cannot be attained' (anu-palambha). It is interesting to note that the same character nien means 'thought' as well as

'moment'. Thoughts are 'moments of consciousness' (**citta-ksana**), without connection to each other. The 'thinking' cannot understand anything, since it is a series of moments, subdivided into arising, staying and ceasing (or disappearing) moments of an inconceivably short duration). These mental moments can be known by the mind, but do not know for themselves. A famous statement of Lin-chi is: 'Do not deceive yourselves: neither at the outside nor at the inside, is there anything whatsoever that you would be able to understand'.

27.   'Form' (**rupa**), in strictly Buddhist terminology signifies the material or physical aspect of the world, its observable material appearance or corporeity, especially the four elements and the five sense organs with their objects.

28.   **Bodhi** is usually translated as 'enlightenment', and as the word **Buddha**, the 'Enlightened One', is derived from the root **budh**: to penetrate, recognize, know, understand, to realize oneself, to awaken. . . It is the ultimate fruit of the path of cultivation.

29.   'Non-arising' or 'un-born' is the judgment of supreme wisdom about whatever exists. This expression does not mean the opposite of 'arising' but, like 'emptiness', 'non-duality', and 'no self-nature', it points toward the absolute truth concerning reality, which transcends the relativity of thinking (in terms of being and non-being, created and non-created, eternal and transitory. . .). This theme is the cornerstone of the Great Vehicle and is repeatedly emphasized in the

Lankāvatāra sūtra, (abbr. LAVS), where we for instance read: "Birth is non-birth when it is recognized that the world that presents itself before us is no more than Mind itself." (D.T. Suzuki, The Lankāvatāra sūtra, p. 96).

30. **To nourish the sacred embryo** or 'to mature in the sacred womb' are expressions of the gradual practice, namely of letting the bodhisattva-mind grow to the full maturity of Buddhahood. At the time of sudden awakening it is as if a new human being is conceived, which as an embryo still has to grow, and has to be nourished and protected. (See for example the same expression in T. 245, vol. 8, p. 826b).

31. **Kalpa** is a cosmic period, an 'eternity'; it is often used in connection with the original error, the state of ignorance, which precedes all other states of alienation, and is therefore also often called 'beginningless'.

32. The <u>Vimalakīrti-nirdeśa</u> (T. 475, vol. 14, p. 545a).

33. "The samādhi which is like the images in the ocean" (F.H. Cook, <u>Hua-yen</u> Buddhism, pp. 73-74), also called 'ocean mirror **samādhi**': as the surface of the sea reflects all forms, in the same way a bodhisattva's **samādhi** reflects all truths'. According to the Hua-yen school, the Buddha was in the **samādhi** when he pronounced the <u>Avatamsaka sūtra</u>. The basic idea of this sutra is the unobstructed mutual penetration of all phenomena, and of each phenomena with reality. The Buddha's wisdom is like the ocean in which all dharmas are reflected.

"The so-called Ocean Mirror [is a metaphor

that] symbolizes the innate Buddha Mind.
When [the manifold] illusions are exhausted within, the mind will become serene,
limpid, [and unruffled,] and the infinite
reflections of all 'phenomena will appear
at one time. . ."
(Garma C. C. Chang. The Buddhist Teaching
of Totality, p. 125).

34. The 'mind of the saint' is one of the key expressions in Seng-chao, whose commentary on the Vimalakīrti-nirdeśa was very well known among the
Ch'an masters of this period. The 'mind of the
saint' performs the function of prajñā, sacred or
absolute knowledge, which 'reflects' or intuitively contemplates knowlege. The opposite of 'sacred
knowledge' is erring knowledge which imagines
characters and things, which are not real.

35. The master-disciple relationship is essential in
each spiritual tradition, and is also of central
importance in Ch'an Buddhism. Kalyānamitra literally means 'good, virtuous friend or counselor';
it indicates that in Buddhism one has to rely on
one's own powers, and all that a teacher is able
to do, is to inspire and offer guidance in a
relationship of friendship.

36. Under his explanation and to be suddenly awakened
(tun wu) are Ch'an expressions to indicate the
'sudden' awakening of a disciple. The terms
'gradual' and 'sudden' occur in the Lankāvatāra
sūtra; in the Vimalakīrti-nirdeśa we find a similar expression, which frequently appears in Ch'an
texts: 'at the same moment he suddenly recovered
the original nature'. (T. 475, vol. 14, p. 541a).

37. Again from the Vimalakīrti-nirdeśa: after Vimala-

kīrti has demonstrated how a bodhisattva is in-the-world but not of-the-world, he asks Mañjuśrī why being in-the-world is the seed of enlightenment. He answers that he who has gained 'insight in nirvāna' and dwells in 'the correct stage', is no longer capable of reaching true enlightenment (because he mistakes his insight and stage for enlightenment). He, however, who has a sense of self as high as Mount Sumeru is still capable, just like a lotus cannot grow on a high plateau but can grow in marshes. Thereupon Mahākāśyapa says: 'Indeed, we are no longer able to become enlightened, like a śrāvaka, who has broken his ties with existence, and is no longer interested in true enlightenment. Therefore the ordinary person is still susceptible, the śrāvaka not.' (T. 475, vol. 14, p. 549b).

38. **Dharma-nature** is a Mahāyāna concept which indicates the true state of all things, implying the ultimate source and condition of all phenomena (**dharmatā**).

39. **To reflect** points to the functioning of the 'holy' mind, which as wisdom or absolute knowledge intuitively sees the truth, or reflects it as a mirror. Hui-neng also uses this expression: When somebody asked him about the secret of his teaching he said: 'What I teach you through my words, is not the secret at all. If you look inside, you will find the secret on your side'. Similar classical expressions, like also 'to reflect inward onto one's own substance' often occur in the writings of Ch'an masters and derive their terminology from Taoism. 'Water in tranquillity is so clear that it even reflects the hairs of

beard and eyebrows. How much more, then, the tranquillity of the sage (or saint), mirror of heaven and earth, which reflects all things in their multiplicity.' (Chuang-tzu).

40. 'As numerous as the grains of sand in the river Ganges' is an image found in the LAVS for the Buddha's teaching: it can be explained in an infinite number of ways but never exhaustively or completely. The Buddhist scriptures contain many symbolical phrases, which in their exaggerated quantitative expression, suggest a new qualitative dimension.

41. When a śrāvaka approaches the relative nirvāna, he disposes of supernatural powers and is able to perform certain physical transformations. He can stop his existence in the three worlds by entering into the 'flame-samādhi' which destroys body and mind. The nirvāna thus attained is, however, a sterile emptiness, like ashes which are totally extinguished by water. The bodhisattva's true emptiness, is, in contrast, dynamic.

42. This is a stereotyped end-formula in Ch'an in-structions. As a way of diversion after the long meditation sessions, one stands during the in-struction, in contrast to other Buddhist schools, where sitting is the prescribed posture.

43. By defilements, or to become defiled, one under-stands the three fundamental motivations or roots of existence: desire, hatred and ignorance, with which all psychic problems or 'conflicting emo-tions (kleśa) are linked.

44. Vimalakīrti describes the attitude of a bodhi-sattva who liberates the world. He indicates that he neither controls his thoughts, as a śrāvaka

does, nor gives free reins to his mind, as fools do. "To act neither as an ordinary person nor as a saint, such is the bodhisattva's way of action. Neither to commit impure actions, nor to achieve pure actions, such is the bodhisattva's way of life." (T. 475, vol. 14, p. 545b).

45. Vimalakīrti says: "There is a teaching method called the **inexhaustible lamp**. One and the same lamp can light a hundred thousand lamps, without losing its own brightness. Similarly, a bodhisattva enlightens hundreds of thousands of beings, without weakening his own enlightenment". (T. 475, vol. 14, p. 543b). The analogy of the lamp also points to the Ch'an tradition, in which the succession of patriarchs or the transmission of the teaching about the mind-ground is called the 'transmission of the lamp'.

    In Nan-yüeh's biography we read in connection with Ma-tsu's succession: 'How could the transmission of the one lamp be exhaustive?' (SKSC, T. 2081, vol. 50, p. 761b).

46. A quotation from the Sūtra in Forty-two Chapters. 'Who says farewell to his parents and leaves the family, discerns the mind, penetrates unto the basis and understands the doctrine of **wu-wei** (the unconditioned, lit.: 'no-action') is called śramana (t. 784, vol. 17, p. 722). 'Śramana' is the designation for a Buddhist monk in general.

47. To posit is to create appellations, it is the conceptual verbalization of reality: for instance, **bodhi** and **nirvāna** are conceptualizations of Buddhism, 'God', 'essence' and 'energy' are conceptualizations in the respective areas of religion, philosophy and physics.

48. The following themes all occur in The Awakening of Faith.

49. A Chinese interpretation of the Buddha's name 'Śākyamuni'.

50. A sentence from the Golden Light sutra is often cited in Ch'an texts: 'The true Dharma-kāya of the Buddha is as empty space, and manifests forms corresponding to the beings, as the moon in water.' (T. 663, vol. 16, p. 344b).

51. "There is a teaching method toward emancipation which is called Finite and Infinite. Finite is called the conditioned and Infinite the unconditioned. The bodhisattva does not exhaust the conditioned and does not dwell in the unconditioned" (VKN, T. 475, vol. 14, p. 554b). In other words, the bodhisattva does not destroy the conditioned dharmas to attach himself to the unconditioned, as the śrāvaka does.

52. VKN, T. 475, vol. 14, p. 538a.

53. "What do you think, Śāriputra, does the rising of the bright sun go together with darkness?. . . the bodhisattva makes the bright wisdom shine forth,. . . and dissipates the contaminations of all beings." (VKN, T. 475, vol. 14, p. 555b).

54. The non-arising is a basic tenet of Mahāyāna Buddhism. The doctrine, or the observation of the non-arising of dharmas presupposes a 'patient acceptance'. Traditionally three degrees of 'patience' are distinguished (see DCBT, p. 65): it grows from a purely verbal conviction toward acceptance and finally reaches perfect forbearance and total recognition. This is the highest spiritual achievement of a bodhisattva. 'Not to say anything about any dharma, to explain nothing, to

demonstrate nothing and to know nothing, to ex-
clude every question and answer, that is to enter
into non-duality.' Then Vimalakīrti was asked to
explain in turn the doctrine of non-duality.
Vimalakīrti remained silent. . . . Thereupon five
thousand bodhisattvas received the acceptance of
non-arising". (VKN, T. 475, vol. 14, p. 551c).

55. See Preface p. 7, note 8.

56. Hsi-t'ang Chih-tsang (735-814) was a disciple of
Ching-shan Fa-ch'in (see section 27) of the Niu-
t'ou school. Hence his name 'hsi-t'ang' ('western
hall'): it is the hall where the newly arrived
ones and the guests were accommodated, in contrast
with the 'eastern hall', which was reserved to the
elders and the hosts. According to tradition
Hsi-t'ang was the most prestigious of Ma-tsu's
disciples.

Pai-chang Huai-hai (720-814) was likewise one
of the most important successors of Ma-tsu, and
pioneer of the monastic rule which made the Ch'an
movement into an independent school. His original
monastic code: "The Pure Regulations of Pai-
chang" has not survived, but is known through
later versions. His tomb inscription has been
preserved, as well as several collections of his
recorded sayings. He was the master of Huang-po
(Lin-chi's master) and has been incorporated as
the second of four masters in the Ssu-chia yü-lu,
whereby he is recognized as an official successor
of Ma-tsu.

Nan-ch'üan P'u-yüan (748-834) became later the
most famous of Ma-tsu's successors. The Pi-yen lu
contains six kung-an of his and the Wu-men kuan
four. His recorded sayings have been partially
perserved.

57. During the conversation the long sleeves were folded over the wrist. At the end, or as a sign of disagreement of disapproval, the sleeve was shaken down before one left.

58. In fact Ma-tsu approved of the two answers: **Tsang** (**pitaka** or 'basket', term for the Buddhist canon of scriptures), expresses the principle, the doctrine or theory; whereas **Hai** ('sea', image of **samādhi**) expresses phenomena, meditation, practice. P'u-yüan who knows how to express himself in a 'transcendent' way, has been added later because of rivalry among the successors of Ma-tsu's three foremost disciples.

59. The word 'pot' is also jokingly used for 'body'. The Ch'üan-teng lu adds that the other monks did not dare to ask any further questions.

60. Ta-chu Hui-hai's (of unknown dates) family name was **Chu**, to which 'great pearl' (**ta chu**) alludes. He first was a disciple of Tao-chih in Ta-yün ssu ('Great Cloud Temple') of Yüeh-chou, to the southeast of Hang-chou in the province of Chekiang. After his training period with Ma-tsu he returned to Tao-chih. Later he disappeared from the world and pretended insanity, thus the CTL, whereas in reality he composed the Tun-wu yao-men. Several recorded sayings of his circulated, which have not all been incorporated in this work. The present Tun-wu yao-men consists of two 'scrolls', of which the first one was only discovered and published during the Ming dynasty (1369). The second 'scroll' consists of two parts, the first of which is probably the work mentioned here: the chapter about Hui-hai in scroll 6 of the CTL; it corresponds with the Tsu-t'ang chi and the Tsung-ching

lu and is thus based on an older source. (HTC
110, pp. 420-433a, translated by John Blofeld, The
Zen Teaching of Hui-hai).

61. The coming of Bodhidharma from India, viz. the
meaning of Ch'an Buddhism. It is a stereotyped
question in Ch'an dialogues, which serves as an
abstract and discursive pretext to elicit a direct
reaction, like the question about the essence of
Buddhism in section 7.

62. In other words: 'I won't tell you in the presence
of a third party' (Bodhidharma?)

63. The dharma hall is the principal building in a
Ch'an monastery, where instructions were given; in
other schools it was called 'discourse hall' or
'hall of interpretation'.

64. Shih-kung was a fearful disciple of Ma-tsu, who
had always bow and arrow at hand to shoot at
'man'. Lin-chi considers him as one of his predecessors, a pioneer of the Hung-chou School.
Besides being a hunter, he was also a famous poet.

65. To cut off one's hair is tantamount to becoming a
monk.

66. To herd the ox is a well-known imagery of the
growth process in Ch'an training. See for instance "The Verses Illustrating the Ten Ox Pic-
tures", HTC 113, pp. 459-471, which have been
translated by D. T. Suzuki, Manual of Zen Buddhism, pp. 127-144, and others.

67. These are concepts in Indian logic, adopted by
Buddhism to point out the insufficiency of each
logical statement concerning ultimate truth. The
basic alternatives are: being and non-being, i.e.
affirmation and negation. Here two more alternatives may follow by affirming or negating both of

them: both being and non-being; and: neither
being nor non-being. In Ch'an texts the four
assertions are also: oneness, diversity, being
and non-being.

The hundred negations are deducted therefrom by
applying each of the four alternatives to the four
assertions. These 16 assertions are then considered in the present, the past and the future;
these 48 further in the condition of 'already
arisen' or 'not yet arising'. To these 96 are
finally added the four original alternatives. In
the Ch'an school the hundred negations also mean
the series of statements about the mind, which is
'neither this nor that, neither inside nor outside' etc.: the well-known **neti, neti** of Hindu
philosophy complemented a hundredfold.

Ch'an master Yung-chia says about the impossi-
bility of reaching insight by logical thinking:
"the mind affirms neither being nor non-being; the
mind negates neither being nor non-being. If one
affirms being or non-being, one is caught in the
trap of affirmation; if one negates being or
non-being, one is caught in the trap of negation."
(T. 2013, vol. 48, p. 391c)
68. (Chih-) tsang is Hsi-t'ang and Hai is Pai-chang
from section 5.
69. **Nirvāna** (see Introduction, p. 19; note 2) is
neither absence nor presence. It is the 'only
reality' (also called 'living water') which neither arises nor ceases, neither remains nor goes
on as a river flows by and yet remains. Once
Confucius stood by a river and said: 'It passes
just like this and does not cease day or night'
(<u>Lun-yü</u>, IX, 16).

70. Fa-ch'ang is usually called **Ta-mei** (large plum), according to the mountain where he resided (in the province of Chekiang). His Recorded Sayings are presumably the oldest text of the Hung-chou School.
71. In the Ch'an school it was the unwritten rule that one could withdraw to the mountains only after 'understanding the mind and seeing one's nature'.
72. Of this encounter, the SKSC gives a more extensive report, based on the historic memorial of Wu-yeh (See Introduction, pp. 66-68).
73. The Vehicles of the śrāvaka; the **pratyekabuddha** or one who attains enlightenment through his own efforts and for his own benefit only; and the **bodhisattva**.
74. **Teng** is the family name of Ch'an master Wu-t'ai Yin-feng, a lay disciple of Ma-tsu. **Shih-t'ou** Hsi-ch'ien is the famous contemporary of Ma-tsu. (See Introduction, pp. 35-36).
75. A monk's **staff** (khakkhara) had at the top metal rings for shaking and was used to announce one's arrival or to keep at a distance wild animals on the road.
76. For an interpretation of this dialogue, see Introduction, pp. 65-66.
77. An image derived from the LAVS, which originally reads as follows: "As a fool who looks at the finger when the moon is pointed out, so is he who attaches himself to concepts and terms and does not see my true reality. The mind (citta) dances as a dancer, consciousness (**manas**) is like a jester, knowledge in the company of five (vijñāna) creates the objective world as a stage" (T. 670, vol. 16, p. 510c).

78. An image found in the <u>Hua-yen</u> <u>sutra</u> (T. 278, vol. 9, p. 607c).

79. P'ang-yün chü-shih (ca. 740-808). Many recorded sayings of his have been preserved (See R. F. Sasaki, trans., <u>The</u> <u>Recorded</u> <u>Sayings</u> <u>of</u> <u>Layman</u> <u>P'ang</u>). The word 'layman' (upāsaka) indicates a Buddhist who does not become a monk but remains in the world as 'master of the family', in contrast with 'religious', someone who 'leaves the family'.

80. In the <u>Lotus</u> <u>sūtra</u> the Buddha says that all his instructions are only teaching devices (**dharma-paryāya**) and skillful means of salvation (upāya), as with an empty fist crying children can be pacified. In the <u>Nirvāna</u> <u>sūtra</u> as well this comparison occurs: "When a child cries, his parents take yellow poplar leaves and say: 'Do not cry, do not cry! We are giving you gold.' The child sees the leaves and takes them for gold." (T. 374, vol. 12, p. 485a). This comparison is often cited by the Ch'an masters. For instance Huang-po says: 'Things like **bodhi** and so on do not really exist. Whatever the Tathāgata said about them, was only to convert people, exactly like yellow leaves are taken for gold to make children stop crying.' (T. 2012, vol. 48, p. 386c).

81. Tan-yuan-chen received the tradition of 'drawing a circle' from his master Nan-yang Hui-chung (died in 776). He and his master are mainly famous for their conversations with emperor Tai-tsung (r. 763-780).

82. It was a general custom among Ch'an monks to wander for many years in search for masters who could help them to 'become a Buddha'.

83. Drawing a circle (lit.: 'perfect character') symbolizes the nature of enlightened consciousness.
This method was developed under the influence of
the Hua-yen School and was later also adopted by
the Kui-yang School, while rejected by the other
Ch'an schools.

84. In order to see 'sparks' (or 'flowers in the
sky'), to see strange things or to create illusions, in other words, to delude oneself for
instance by deliberate religious or 'enlightened'
behaviour.

85. Ching-shan Fa-ch'in (714-792) was a disciple of
Ma-tsu (Ho-lin Hsüan-su, 668-752) and a successor
of the Niu-t'ou School. Mount Ching is located
near Hang-chou in Chekiang province, and became an
important centre of Ch'an Buddhism, especially of
the Lin-chi School.

86. **Chung Kuo-shih**, National or Imperial Preceptor
Chung, is the title of Nan-yang Hui-chung, master
of Tan-yüan (see note 82).

87. The 'lion' is a symbol of the Buddha expounding
the doctrine.

88. "the Tathāgata is neither to go out nor to enter"
(VKN, T. 475, vol. 14, p. 555a).

89. Yao-shan Wei-yen (died in 834) is known for his
humor. Remarkable in this dialogue is that both
Shih-t'ou and Ma-tsu give him a similar answer.

90. The Twelve Divisions of the Mahāyāna canons are:
   (i)   sūtra, Buddha's discourse
   (ii)   geya, metrical piece
   (iii) gāthā, chant or poem
   (iv)   nidāna, statement of subject matter; sum-
          mary
   (v)   itivrttaka, narrative

(vi)   **jātaka**, former life story
(vii)   **abhidharma**, treatise
(viii) **avadāna**, parable, story
(ix)   **upadeśa**, instruction
(x)   **udāna**, impromptu address
(xi)   **vaipulya**, expanded sutra
(xii)   **vyākarana**, prophecy
(See DCBT, p. 44 and p. 19)

91. In order to benefit or to 'ferry across' other sentient beings. To establish oneself on a mountain did not merely signify withdrawal from the world to live a life of meditation, it also meant to gather disciples and to found a monastery. Mount Yao, where Yao-shan Wei-yen established himself, is situated in Hunan province.

92. Tan-hsia (739-824) was a Confucian and, as Yao-shan, also a disciple of Shih-t'ou. He is famous for the burning of a Buddha statue.

93. In the meditation hall there most often was a statue of Mañjuśrī, the bodhisattva symbolizing wisdom.

94. A religious name was traditionally given at the occasion of religious vows.

95. The knowing and seeing of the Buddha is the Buddha consciousness. "If in knowing and seeing there still is room for knowing, it is the root of ignorance; if knowing and seeing are without seeing, it is nirvana, pure reality without contamination". (Śūrangama sūtra).

96. Mount Nan-Yüeh (Southern Peak) was the centre of Ts'ao-hsi Hui-neng's successors.

97. The Eastern lake is today's Tung-t'ing lake in Hunan province.

98. Tao-wu Yüan-chih (769-835) and Yün-yen T'an-sheng

(780-841) were brothers and successors of Yao-shan (See Section 30). Tung-shan Liang-chieh (807-869) was a disciple of Yün-yen and founder of the Ts'ao-Tung (Jap.: Soto) School. This is a typical commentary of the later kung-an literature.

BIBLIOGRAPHY

The following list is restricted to a number of translations of classical Buddhist texts related to Ch'an Buddhism. The authors' names are in fact the names of the translators-annotators.

More complete bibliographies are found in the work of P. Yampolski, The Platform Sutra of the Sixth Patriarch (q.v.) and in P. Beautrix, Bibliographie du Bouddhisme Zen, 2 vols., Brussels: Institut Belge des Hautes Études Bouddhiques, 1969 and 1975.

BLOFELD, J. The Zen Teaching of Huang-po. London: The Buddhist Society, 1968.

BLOFELD, J. The Zen Teaching of Hui-hai. London: Rider, 1962.

CHAN, Wing-tsit. The Platform Scripture (Asian Institute Translations, no. 3). New York: St. John's University Press, 1963.

CHANG, Chung-yüan. Original Teachings of Ch'an Buddhism. New York: Pantheon, 1970.

CLEARY, T. and J.C. The Blue Cliff Records, 3 vols. London-Berkeley: Shambhala, 1977.

CONZE, E. Buddhist Wisdom Books. London: Allen & Unwin, 1958.

DEMIÉVILLE, P. Les Entretiens de Lin-tsi. Paris: Fayard, 1972.

GUNDERT, W. Bi Yan Lu, 3 vols. Münich: C. Hansor Verlag, 1960-73.

HAKEDA, Y.S. The Awakening of Faith. New York-London: Columbia University Press, 1967.

HURVITZ, L. Scripture of the Lotus Blossom of the Fine Dharma. New York: Columbia University Press, 1976.

LAMOTTE, É.   L'Enseignement de Vimalakīrti.   Louvain:
Éditions Peeters, 1962.

LAMOTTE, É.   Le Traité de la Grande Vertu de Sagesse, 5
vols.   Louvain: Éditions Peeters, 1966-.

LU, K'uan-yü (Charles LUK),   Ch'an and Zen Teaching,   3
vols.   London: Rider, 1960-69.

LU, K'uan-yü.   The Surangama Sutra.   London: Rider,
1973.

LU, K'uan-yü.   The Transmission of the Mind.   London:
Rider, 1974.

LUK, C. (LU K'uan-yü).   The Vimalakīrti Nirdeśa Sutra.
Berkeley: Shambhala, 1972.

MURANO, S.   The Lotus Sutra.   Tokyo, 1974.

SASAKI, R.   F. and   others.   The   Recorded Sayings   of
Layman P'ang.   New York-Tokyo: Wheatherhill, 1971.

SEKIDA, K.   Two   Zen   Classics.   New   York-Tokyo:
Wheatherhill, 1977.

THURMAN, R.   The Holy Teachings of Vimalakīrti.   Phil-
adelphia: Pennsylvania   State   University   Press,
1976.

YAMAMOTO, K.   The   Mahaparinirvana   Sutra,   3   vols.
Tokyo: Karinbunko, 1973-75.

YAMPOLSKI, P.   The   Platform Sutra of the Sixth Patriarch.   New York: Columbia University Press, 1967.

INDEX

sūtra(s)   39, 70
Sūtra of Buddha-names   50

T   Ta-chu   93
Tan-yüan   103
Tao (see Path)
Tathāgata 63, 77
Tathāgata-garbha 63, 91
Teng Yin-feng   99
T'ien-jan (Tan-hsia)   107
Ts'ao-tung school (Soto)   57
Tsu-t'ang chi   34, 39, 76, 111, 113, 126
tsung (school)   69
Tsung-ching lu   76, 111
Tsung-mi   31, 33, 36, 40, 45, 74
Tun-wu yao-men   126
Tung-ssu   40

V   Vimalakīrtinirdeśa   9, 46, 52, 54, 77, 79, 119, 120
Vinaya 39, 70

W   Wei-chien   95
Wei-yen (Yao-shan)   105-7, 131-2
Wu-chiu   65-66, 100
Wu-men kuan   77, 125
Wu-yeh   66, 67, 98

Y   Yogācārabhūmi-śāstra   52
Yung-chia   6, 21, 55

Z   **Zen** (see **Ch'an**)

STUDIES IN ASIAN THOUGHT AND RELIGION